The Old Beloved Path

Fire Ant Books

The Old Beloved Path

Daily Life among the Indians
of the Chattahoochee River Valley

William W. Winn

Published by The University of Alabama Press in cooperation with
The Historic Chattahoochee Commission and The Columbus Museum

First paperback printing 2008 by
The University of Alabama Press
Tuscaloosa, Alabama 35487-0380

∞
The paper on which this book is printed meets the minimum requirements of
American National Standard for Information Science — Permanence of Paper for
Printed Library Materials, ANSI Z39.48-1984.

Cataloging-in-Publication Data available from the Library of Congress

"Fire Ant Books"

ISBN 978-0-8173-5520-3 (pbk. : alk. paper)

Do not attempt to eat the plants described in this book unless you are accompa-
nied by an expert. Misidentification can lead to serious illness and even death.
Many people have become ill after eating supposedly safe vegetation.
—The Author

For the Creek People

and

For Frank Schnell for whom the
mute stones speak,

and

For J. P. DuVernet, who hears the singing fire

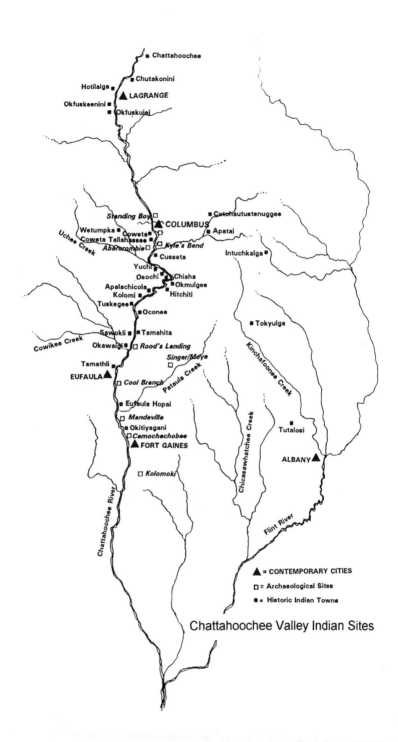

■ Chattahoochee

■ Chutakonini

Hotilaiga ■

▲ LAGRANGE

Okfuskeenini ■

■ Okfuskujai

Standing Boy □

Cotohautustenuggee ■

▲ COLUMBUS

Wetumpka ■

■ Coweta

■ Apatai

Uchee Creek

Coweta Tallahassee ■

Abercrombie □

Kyle's Bend □

■ Cusseta

Intuchkalga ■

Yuchi ■

Osochi ■

■ Chiaha

Apalachicola ■

■ Okmulgee

Kolomi ■

Hitchiti ■

Tuskegee ■

■ Oconee

■ Tokyulga

Sawokli ■ ■ ■ Tamahita

Cowikee Creek

Okawaigi ■ □ Rood's Landing

Singer/Moye

Kinchafoonee Creek

Tamathli ■

□

EUFAULA ▲

□ Cool Branch

Patsula Creek

■ Eufaula Hopai

□ Mandeville

■ Okitiyagani

□ Cemochechobee

▲ FORT GAINES

Tutalosi ■

Chicasawhatchee Creek

ALBANY ▲

□ Kolomoki

Chattahoochee River

Flint River

▲ = CONTEMPORARY CITIES

□ = Archaeological Sites

■ = Historic Indian Towns

Chattahoochee Valley Indian Sites

Illustrations by Cheryl Mann Hardin
with plant drawings by Faith Birkhead

Cover art by Joe Belt

TABLE OF CONTENTS

LIST OF MYTHS

FOREWORD

This publication has been produced jointly by the Columbus Museum and the Historic Chattahoochee Commission. It is appropriate that our two organizations have collaborated on this project, as both are committed to the study and preservation of the cultural heritage of the Chattahoochee River Valley region. Accredited by the American Association of Museums, the Museum is a non-profit corporation chartered in the state of Georgia and jointly operated by a Board of Trustees and the Muscogee County School District. Originally opened to the public in 1954, the Museum was expanded and renovated in 1989 to become by far the largest museum in the Southeast to focus on American art and history and is unique in its concentration on the art and history of the Southeast in general and on the Chattahoochee River Valley area in particular.

Organized in 1970, the Historic Chattahoochee Commission is charged with the responsibility of promoting tourism and historic preservation throughout 18 counties located in the lower Chattahoochee River Valley. Since 1978 the Commission has operated under an interstate compact co-sponsored by Alabama and Georgia, and it is the only tourism and preservation agency in the nation officially sanctioned to cross state lines.

Responsibility for the development of *The Old Beloved Path* has been shared equally between our two organizations. The Commission provided funding to produce the manuscript, while the Museum funded printing and other production costs. Essential for the completion of the project was the Museum's Wehle Fund, established for the express purpose of publishing a history of our region.

The Old Beloved Path is a study of the various means which the native peoples of the Chattahoochee region used to subsist from the land. It describes the plants they gathered and

xi

cultivated, the animals they hunted, and other materials they collected for food, clothing, shelter, and tools. It describes a culture that flourished here for centuries and that was a primary contributor to the frontier experience that is our region's historical legacy. It is hoped that the present volume will be the first in a series of texts that will explore a variety of historical topics relevant to our region.

It is with great pleasure that we again present *The Old Beloved Path*. We hope that it will foster increased appreciation for the complexity and richness of the cultural heritage of the Chattahoochee River Valley Region.

Charles T. Butler
Director
The Columbus Museum

Douglas Clare Purcell
Executive Director
Historic Chattahoochee
Commission

ACKNOWLEDGMENTS

So many people have contributed to the making of *The Old Beloved Path* that the author hesitates to list them lest he inadvertently leave someone out. However, I want especially to thank the members of the editorial board of the Chattahoochee Valley Legacy Series: Fred Fussell, former curator of the Columbus Museum; Douglas Purcell, executive director of the Historic Chattahoochee Commission; Frank Schnell, archaeologist for the Columbus Museum; John Lupold of Columbus College; Jerry Brown, professor of journalism at Auburn University; and F. Clason Kyle.

The illustrations in the text were done by Cheryl Mann Hardin and Faith Birkhead, without whose talent and hard work these pages would be barren, indeed.

Thanks also go to Joe Mahan, then of the Columbus Museum, now of the Lower Chattahoochee Regional Development Center, for encouraging the author many years ago to look into the lives of the native inhabitants of the Chattahoochee River Valley.

Of course, anyone who writes about the daily life of Southeastern Indians, particularly the Creeks, works in the shadow of the late John R. Swanton, the Smithsonian anthropologist whose original research on Southeastern Indians, particularly the Muskogulgi or "Creeks," remains the scholarly bedrock upon which so much subsequent work in the field has been based. My debt to Swanton is happily acknowledged in the bibliography at the end of this book.

Much of the practical information found in the text was developed or tested on wilderness excursions throughout the Southeast and in the Chattahoochee River Valley itself. From among numerous persons with whom I have shared campfires over the years--not always with this book in mind but always with it in my heart--I must thank James DuVernet, Kay DuVernet, Paul Hemphill, William "Bucky" Parker, Frank O'Neill, Philip Carter, Jack Lange, Henry Ball, Tscharner Dickerson, and Bob Bracewell.

For patiently demonstrating techniques of Indian woodcraft, I would like to thank Ben Warren Kirkland of Chehaw Park in Albany, Georgia; Preston Roberts of Hayes, North Carolina; Thomas White of Rydal, Georgia; and Driver Pheasant of Cherokee, North Carolina. Kirkland was particularly helpful.

Thanks also to Gary White Deer from Ada, Oklahoma, for a wonderful and informative evening on the Chattahoochee River discussing the medicinal and spiritual properties of certain Indian plants.

Jerry Brown read the text and suggested many improvements. Mary-Margaret Bowles did heroic work on both the text and the bibliography. The book would not be publishable without her efforts. John Lupold saw the manuscript through numerous revisions and sets of proofs. Thanks also to Jeff Davison for his careful editing. Pat Drake of the Columbus College history department patiently made the necessary corrections and indexed the text. The facilities of the Columbus College Computer Center were kindly placed at the disposal of the editors. Mike Owen did the page layout. Joan Emens, Head of the Reference Department of the W. C. Bradley Memorial Library, and Charlotte Kennedy, Reference Associate, found rare books and obscure papers that were of great benefit in the research. F. Clason Kyle paid for much of the research on which *The Old Beloved Path* is based and also read the manuscript.

My long-suffering wife, Elinor, typed long sections of the book and the bibliography and put up with some rather strange behavior on my part while *The Old Beloved Path* was in preparation. I don't see how or why she does it. Victoria Bracewell and Michael Dickerson lent moral support.

I am grateful also to the publishers of *The Atlanta Journal* and the *Columbus Ledger-Enquirer* for giving me permission to use material that first appeared in those newspapers.

And finally, I would like to say that Frank Schnell, archaeologist at the Columbus Museum, has forgotten more about the Indians of the Chattahoochee River Valley than the author will ever know. Schnell not only provided books and research materials upon which much of the text is based, but he also read and criticized the text and was a constant source of encouragement throughout the project. Without his help, there would have been no *The Old Beloved Path*. The errors contained in the book are, however, my own.

INTRODUCTION

The world of the Indians of the Chattahoochee River Valley no longer exists. It has been obliterated by the plow, the ax and saw, the bulldozer and road machine, the technology that allows mankind to construct massive dams of concrete and steel, and by an industrial economy that requires people to live in cities, a process we have come to call, rather euphemistically, "urbanization."

Where there were once vast forests of towering oaks and hickories and poplars that reddened and yellowed the Valley hills in the autumn and provided deep, cool shade in the summer, there are now monotonous carpets of loblolly and slash pines--or raw red hillsides barren of any trees at all. Where there were once cypress swamps and swamp chestnut oaks and shadowy thickets of persimmon and gum trees, there are now dry, flat fields of soybeans and cotton interspersed with auto graveyards, juke joints, and trailer parks.

Where game trails and Indian foot paths--often one and the same--ran beside the Chattahoochee and followed burbling creeks winding through the majestic wilderness, there are now four-lane expressways and hardtops on which glassy-eyed local commuters and Florida-bound tourists compete for road space with massive 18-wheelers, crazily ladened logging trucks, road graders, and lumbering farm machinery.

Beaver ponds and oxbow lakes that provided shelter and food for thousands of migratory waterfowl and for fish, frogs, turtles, alligators, and hosts of other reptiles, amphibians, and birds have vanished from the earth, drained and back-filled to make room for shopping centers, office parks, and suburban real estate developments.

Gone forever from the Valley are the night scream of the panther, the blood-curdling howl of the wolf, the raucous hammering of the ivory-billed woodpecker, the shadow that would pass over the land as clouds of migrating passenger pigeons soared overhead toward their roosts.

Chalala, *Ivory-billed woodpecker*

The very waters of the earth have been broken to the will of the white man so that they flow or cease flowing according to his will. The falls at Columbus and Phenix City, where the Indians of Coweta and Cusseta would go every spring to fish, are no more, obliterated by the turgid backwaters of the mill dams. Just above the lower dams are even larger dams and more extensive backwaters, artificial impoundments whose depths cover the campsites and rock the bones of wandering bands of hunters who found their way to the Chattahoochee at the end of the last Ice Age. Below Eufaula at Fort Gaines, Columbia, and Bainbridge, massive locks and dams throttle the river again, creating reservoirs the size of inland seas and covering the villages and remains of a people whose civilization was ancient when the first European set foot in the New World.

And yet....

It is almost impossible to grow up in the Chattahoochee River Valley and not encounter some evidence of the Native American people who lived here for at least 12,000 years, from roughly 10,000 B.C. until they were forcibly removed to the American West in the 1830s. The very name Chattahoochee, a Muskogee Indian word that has been variously interpreted as meaning River of Flowering or Painted Rocks, Red River, and River of the Choctaws, evokes memories of a vanished people.

So do the names of dozens of other streams and creeks in the Valley, among them Upatoi, Uchee, Weracoba, Hannahatchee, Patula, Hatchechubbee, Chewalla, Omusee, Cowikee, Tobannee, Cheneyhatchee, Sawhatchee, Wylaune, Ossahatchi, Ichabuckler, Halloka, Kolomoki, Coheelee, Hodchodkee, Talipahoga, Hitchitee, Ihagee, Oswichee, Cochgalechee, Hallowaka, Bustahatchee, Cemochechobee--to name only a few.

And of the towns and crossroads, many bearing the same names as the creeks, including Cusseta, Uchee, Eufaula, Ossahatchi, Wetumpka, Cataula, Oswichee, Hatchechubbee, Upatoi, Wylaune....

Moreover, there is scarcely a hunter or fisherman, or a boy or girl, who has roamed the woods and fields in the Valley and not come across an "arrowhead" glinting in the grass or a fragment of pottery mingled with the earth. Some more fortunate few have discovered pipe bowls, often carved into fantastic animal shapes, or smooth, disc-shaped stones that were used in the favorite Indian game of *chunkee*, or colorful beads that were an important 17th-century trade item between the Spanish in Florida and the Indians of the lower Chattahoochee River Valley.

Many area museums, and not a few national ones, are filled

with artifacts left behind by these first inhabitants of the Valley. Local archaeologists are constantly digging up artifacts from the remote Indian past, often found in association with the numerous mounds that dot the Valley on both sides of the Chattahoochee from LaGrange and West Point-Lanett south to Columbus-Phenix City, Eufaula, Fort Gaines, Blakely, and Bainbridge. Many Valley school children have visited the well-known Kolomoki mound site near Blakely, now a state tourist attraction, or gone on field trips to Rood's Landing, Singer-Moye, Cemochechobee, Abercrombie, or some of the other undeveloped mound sites in the Valley.

And finally, after decades of neglect, historians are beginning to turn their attention to the frontier days on the river, when white, red, and black men and women lived side by side in an uneasy truce.

Yet, with all this, few inhabitants of the Valley today know much about the Indians who once lived here, especially as concerns their daily life: how they went about gathering food and preparing it for consumption, what was the nature of their religion, social organization, education, recreation, family life, and government. *The Old Beloved Path: Daily Life Among the Indians of the Chattahoochee River Valley* is designed to fill that gap.

The book is divided into three parts. The first part covers what we might call the Early Prehistoric Period, which dates from 10,000 B.C., the approximate date of the oldest clear evidence of mankind in the Chattahoochee River Valley, to the beginning of the Woodland Period in around 1,000 B.C. The Woodland or Middle Period, which lasted to about A.D. 700, was marked by certain technological advances: The discovery of the technique of making pottery, the development of the bow and arrow, a more settled lifestyle, and much more elaborate social and spiritual life. The concluding section, the Late Prehistoric, dates from A.D. 700 to the arrival of the first Europeans in the Valley shortly after 1600. For this last section, which is by far the longest part of the book, I have used historical sources with the intent of describing Indian life just before it was adulterated by European contact.

My aim is to reflect, at all times and in all parts of the book, the daily life of the Indians of the Valley, in as pure a state as I can capture it. The reader is cautioned, therefore, not to pay too much attention to dates in *The Old Beloved Path*. They are less important than the subsistence technologies which underlie the daily lives of the earliest inhabitants of the Valley. These technologies, which disappeared rapidly after European contact, made it possible for the Valley's earliest inhabitants to survive and, beginning from about 1,000 B.C., to establish a rich, complex culture that was both individually satisfying and spiritually rewarding. James Adair, an 18th-century trader who was an astute observer of Southeastern Indians, says the native people of the region referred to their traditional way of life as "the old beloved path." Hence, the name of this book.

A Note of Pronunciation and Spelling

In the interest of making the text more accessible to the general reader, I have attempted to simplify the spelling--and thus pronunciation--of the Muskogee words in *The Old Beloved Path*. For example, most a-sounds in Muskogee, including "v" (the sound of the "u" in "but") and broad "a" (the "a" in "palm"), have been rendered as "a." I hope this does not offend purists. I have retained the letter "k" as it is customarily used in the Creek syllabary, however, as in *thluko* for *thlucco*, *miko* for *mico*, etc. The exception is where altering long-established spellings, usually place-names, would likely confuse rather than help the reader, as if I were to insist on Kawita for the more common Coweta, Kasihta for Cusseta, Kowikee for Cowikee and the like. The difficult voiceless "l" in Muskogee is given as "thl" here--*thluko, thlee*--an approximation at best. The plural and collective noun-ending is usually "*ulgi*," pronounced in English, ul-gee. The letter "g" is always hard in the Creek tongue, as in Muscogee.

Early Prehistoric
10,000 - 1,000 B.C.

In the beginning the waters covered everything. It was said "Who will make the land appear?"

Lock-chew, *the Crawfish, said: "I will make the land appear."*

So he went down to the bottom of the water and began to stir up the mud with his tail and hands. He then brought up the mud to a certain place and piled it up.

The owners of the land at the bottom of the water said:

"Who is disturbing our land?" They kept watch and discovered the Crawfish. Then they came near him, but he suddenly stirred the mud with his tail so they could not see him.

Lock-chew *continued his work. He carried mud and piled it up until at last he held up his hands in the air, and so the land appeared above the water.*

The land was soft. It was said: "Who will spread out the land and make it dry and hard?" Some said: "Ah-yok, the Hawk, should spread out the soft land and make it dry." Others said "Yah-tee, the Buzzard, has larger wings; he can spread out the land and make it dry and hard."

Yah-tee *undertook to spread out and dry the earth. He flew above the earth and spread out his long wings over it. He sailed over the earth; he spread it out. After a long while he grew tired of holding out his wings. He began to flap them, and thus he caused the hills and valleys because the dirt was still soft.*

"Who will make the light?" it was said. It was very dark.

Yohah, *the Star, said, "I will make the light."*

It was so agreed. The Star shone forth. It was light

only near him.

"Who will make more light?" it was said.

Shar-pah, *the Moon, said: "I will make more light."* Shar-pah *made more light, but it was still dark.*

T-cho, *the Sun, said: "You are my children, I am your mother, I will make the light. I will shine for you."*

She went to the east. Suddenly light spread over all the earth. As she passed over the earth a drop of blood fell from her to the ground, and from this blood and earth sprang the first people, the children of the Sun, the Yuchi.

The people wished to find their medicine. A great monster serpent destroyed the people. They cut his head from his body. The next day the body and head were together. They again slew the monster. His head again grew to his body.

Then they cut off his head and placed it on top of a tree, so that the body could not reach it. The next morning the tree was dead and the head was united to the body. They again severed it and put it upon another tree. In the morning the tree was dead and the head and body were reunited.

The people continued to try all the trees in the forest. At last they placed the head over the Tar, *the cedar tree, and in the morning the head was dead. The cedar was alive, but covered with blood, which had trickled down from the head.*

Thus the Great Medicine was found.

Fire was made by boring with a stick into a hard weed.

The people selected a second family. Each member of this family had engraved on his door a picture of the sun.

In the beginning all the animals could talk, and but one language was used. All were at peace. The deer lived in a cave, watched over by a keeper and the people were hungry. He selected a deer and killed it. But finally the deer were set free and roved over the entire earth.

All the animals were set free from man, and names were given to them, so that they could be known.

A Yuchi Tale

I

Paleo Period
10,000 - 8,000 B.C.

Archaeologists believe that the first inhabitants of North America, whom we call Indians because Christopher Columbus mistakenly thought he had discovered the East Indies, came from somewhere to the northwest. Although there is still some disagreement as to precisely where these people originated, most authorities believe that the ancestors of American Indians were Mongoloids from Northwestern Asia who came to America by way of a land bridge across the Bering Strait during the last Ice Age some 20,000 years ago.

We know from archaeological evidence that small bands of wandering hunters reached the Eastern Woodlands of North America by at least 12,000 B.C. They were attracted to the Interior Low Plateau region of the Tennessee and Kentucky highlands where many different species of animals congregated at that area's numerous salt licks. From there nomadic bands appear to have spread in different directions, including southward into what is now Northern Alabama and extreme Northwest Georgia. By 10,000 B.C. or thereabouts, several of these bands found their way onto the bluffs of the Chattahoochee River, possibly by way of one of the river's numerous tributaries that reach westward toward the Tallapoosa River and the Alabama Piedmont, or simply by following the Chattahoochee from North Georgia into the Fall Line region.

The first inhabitants of the Valley rim, who lived in what archaeologists call the Paleo Period, endured an extremely rigorous and primitive existence. They lived toward the end of the Pleistocene Epoch, when ice covered much of the Northern United States and the climate in the Chattahoochee River Valley was much colder and wetter than it is today. The river itself was then a roaring cataract, swollen by the melting ice and by the spring runoff from the snow in the mountains to the north. The Valley floor was probably uninhabitable for humans and most animals for much of this time, and, as a consequence, the hunters usually stuck to the high ridges along the river. Traveling in small bands or families, they were constantly on the move in search of the large animals--mastodons, mammoths, ground sloths, and giant bison--that provided meat and fat for food, skins from which to make clothing, and bones from which to fashion tools. Almost every facet of the daily life of Paleo Indians was organized around hunting. Heavy spears tipped with large "Clovis" points, so named from such points found near Clovis, New Mexico, in 1936, laboriously chipped from flint, chert, or quartz, were the hunters' favorite weapons. Knives were made of the same material as spear points, as were the crude scrapers women used to clean flesh from the animal skins used for clothing. Most often their campsites were in the open where they erected rude huts of bones, sticks, and animal skins to shelter them from the elements. As they became more familiar with the area, the Paleo Indians located shallow caves and rock shelters in which to take refuge from the cold nights.

The first people of the Valley hunted their giant quarry in the forests along the Chattahoochee, returning at night to open-air campsites on the ridges. Lacking even the bow and arrow, which the Valley Indians did not have until A.D. 800-900, they pursued game with heavy spears, ganging up on the larger animals and trying to isolate the youngest or oldest animals, which were easier prey.

Although today we tend to look back upon the Paleo Indians as an extremely primitive people, they were able hunters and they were not without skills and technology, especially in their ability to work wood and stone. Even the manufacture of a point and spear required specialized knowledge that could only have been acquired over a long period of time.

Paleo Spear-Making

To begin, the craftsman used a heavy hammer stone, probably

a smooth river rock, to knock thin flakes off a flint boulder. A smaller hammer stone was then used to shape the flint flake into a crude point with a tip on the shaft end. With a blunt tool (later Indians used a deer antler), the craftsman delivered a sharp blow to the tip, knocking off a long, narrow channel or flute. He repeated this maneuver on the opposite side so that there were grooves or flutes on both sides of the point. To sharpen and finish the point, he then used a pointed piece of bone or antler to pressure-flake the edges. Finally, the base or shaft end of the point was ground smooth with sandstone.

The finished point was not necessarily attached directly to the wooden spear shaft, which was probably much thicker and heavier than is generally imagined, but was often hafted onto a short bone fore-shaft by means of the flutes. The tip of the bone shaft was brought into contact with the base of the point, and two small bone splinters were matched to the flutes on either side of the point so that the ends extended over the bone shaft. The base of the point was wrapped tightly with a cord made of vegetable fiber or animal gut, binding shaft and point together. The bone shaft was then inserted into a hole drilled in the end of the wooden spear shaft, which was probably made from a heavy, dense wood that had been seasoned and then hardened by long exposure to fire.

The bone fore-shaft and wood main-shaft configuration may have been designed to facilitate penetration. Since the bone fore-shaft was of smaller diameter than the main-shaft, it would more easily follow the point through the tough hide and muscle of the Indians' quarry. The smooth shape of the point allowed the spear to be withdrawn quickly and, when necessary, to be thrust into the quarry again and again. Many spears may have been equipped with a detachable fore-shaft and point designed to remain in the quarry while the hunters reloaded another point and shaft and delivered another thrust.

The end product was a surprisingly effective weapon-- provided the hunters could get close enough to their quarry to deliver a blow to a vital spot, a dangerous proposition that required considerable courage and a thorough knowledge of animal habits and behavior. It is believed that Paleo Indians did not so much throw as thrust their heavy spears, perhaps using their own body weight to drive the point home. Two or more men may have handled a single spear.

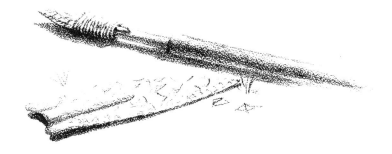

Clovis Points

Roving bands of Paleo Indians were neither large nor numerous, and they seldom stayed in one spot for an extended length of time. As a result, they left few signs of their presence. However, Clovis points, the "signature" of Paleo Indians, have been found on the surface at several places in the Chattahoochee River Valley, including Bartlett's Ferry north of Columbus, on Bull Creek, at Seale, Alabama, and on Fort Benning where Lawson Army Airfield is now located. Clovis points are fairly common elsewhere in Georgia, Alabama, Florida, and throughout the Southeast. Northern Alabama is particularly rich in Clovis sites, of which the so-called Quad site near Decatur is perhaps the best known. Fluted projectile points, differing only slightly from Clovis points, have also been recovered from a Sand Mountain rock shelter in Marshall County, Alabama, near Asbury, and from an ancient campsite on a bluff above the Chattahoochee north of Phenix City.

Wooden spears with fire-hardened points and wooden clubs, knives, and other tools must have also been an important part of Paleo man's hunting gear and weaponry. However, wood rots quickly in the earth, and no trace of such implements dating to prehistoric times has so far been found in the Valley. Bone, also a vital part of early man's tool kit, was used for spear points, scrapers, awls, needles, and as a wood wrench for shaping and straightening wooden spear shafts.

Social Organization

Because we have so few artifacts from the earliest inhabitants of the Valley, our knowledge of their daily life is extremely limited. However, anthropologists who specialize in the study of early American cultures believe the bands must have had some basis of social organization. It is thought that, initially at least, all the members of a given band were related by blood, that is, were members of an extended family or clan. Bands did not marry within, and in time this practice of exogamous marriage established close ties of kinship between bands. At certain times of the year, the bands must have congregated in favorite camps, exchanged ideas and information, arranged marriages, and held ceremonies.

Most likely, each band would have had a leader, especially in the hunt, at this early date a no-nonsense business upon which the very survival of the band and its individual members depended. Some division of labor and some form of organized care of the young, the aged, and the ill would have been necessary. The women cared for the young, made clothing from animal skins, gathered firewood, foraged for wild plant foods, cooked the food over open fires, and looked after what few domestic comforts the band possessed. The men hunted, spent much time making and repairing weapons, and protected the band from its enemies.

Role of the Elders

Since there was no written language, the role of the older band members was extremely important. It was they who passed on the group's essential life knowledge to the young. Instruction was by rote and experience. The young learned by doing and by listening to and imitating their elders. Elders also preserved the band's oral traditions and its history, including tales or myths of its origin, its migratory experiences, and the stories used to instruct the young. It is thought that shamans or medicine men attempted to cure the sick by casting spells or reciting magic formulas.

Although it would perhaps be too much to say that these early people of the Valley had an elaborate religion, it is likely that they believed almost every object--trees, rocks, wild animals, snakes, plants--was possessed with an animating spirit, which could be friendly or unfriendly according to the situation. Perhaps even at this remote time the people of the Valley felt guilt for killing and eating animals. Mankind had to kill and eat animals to live, but in the process he risked angering the animal spirits. We know later Indians of the Valley were deeply concerned about this unavoidable paradox. Thus it was that the historic Creeks, Yuchis, Hitchitis, and other Indians of the area were much preoccupied with propitiating the spirits of the animals they killed lest the collective anger of these spirits overwhelm them. As a result, they had many formulas--we could call them prayers--for appeasing the spirits of slain animals. Before eating any flesh, Indian hunters in historic times always made an offering of a choice piece of any animal they killed, usually throwing it into the fire while reciting a sacrificial formula. Perhaps their remote ancestors during the Paleo Period did the same.

Beyond these few observations, we can say little about the earliest inhabitants of the Valley. They must have been a tough and courageous people or they would not have survived the harsh environment that was their home. But survive they did, for several thousand years. Like people everywhere, they must have loved their mates and doted on their children, known pain and loss, experienced moments of exaltation and spiritual insight, and marveled at the heavens and the mysteries of the universe. All this, however, is speculation. Stones can tell us only so much.

The animals held a meeting, and No-koos-see, *the Bear, presided.*

The question was: how shall day and night be divided? Some desired the day to last all the time; others wanted it always to be night.

After much talk, Chew-thlock-chew, *the Ground Squirrel, said: "I see that* Woot-Kew, *the Raccoon, has rings on his tail divided equally, first a dark color and then a light color. I think day and night should be divided like the rings on the raccoon's tail."*

The animals were surprised at the wisdom of Chew-thlock-chew. *They adopted his plan and divided day and night like the rings on the raccoon's tail, one succeeding the other in regular order.*

No-koos-see *was so envious of* Chew-thlock-chew *that he scratched him and thus caused the stripes on the back of all of his descendants, the ground squirrels.*

A Creek Tale

II

Archaic Period
8,000 - 1,000 B.C.

By around 8,000 B.C., the ice that had covered much of the earth during the Pleistocene Epoch had retreated, and a gradual warming trend was noticeable in the Valley. As the ice melted, the climate changed. By 6,000 B.C., during what climatologists call the Altithermal interval, the air was becoming much less humid, the waters calmer, the Valley drier. The mammoth, mastodon, ground sloth, and giant bison disappeared to be replaced by the white-tailed deer, black bear, raccoon, rabbit, squirrel, gray fox, chipmunk, skunk, porcupine, bobwhite, wild turkey, turtle, and a host of other animals that inhabit the Valley today. Plant life changed also. Pines, oaks, hickories, and a variety of gums became the dominant trees in the forests of the Fall Line region and extended southward along the river and creeks into the upper reaches of the Coastal Plain. Below, in the area now called the Pine Barrens, were towering forests of longleaf or yellow pine (*Pinus palustris*), intermingled with saw palmetto (*Serenoa repens*) and occasional scrub oaks.

These changes were very gradual and took place over hundreds, even thousands, of years. At some time between 4,000-3,000 B.C., the climate stabilized and came to resemble that which we know today. As this occurred, the floor of the Valley became more habitable, the waters receded from the terraces along the river, and the river and its rich food resources became more available to man. Archaeologists call the people who inhabited the Valley during this time the Archaic Indians.

Standing Boy Flint Industry

We know Archaic man was in the Valley because there is clear evidence of his occupation in the area just north of present-day Columbus where Lake Oliver is now located. There in

1959, on a sandy knoll on the north bank of Standing Boy Creek in an area now covered by the waters of the lake, archaeologists found numerous ancient artifacts flaked from a light-colored, heavily weathered flint. Among these were endscrapers, unifacial and bifacial knives, and small, triangular, beveled and notched knives, originally thought to be projectile points, called spinner points by collectors. The flaking done to create the tools is of such a nature as to suggest a highly specialized approach, one reason archaeologists believe the site was the location of what is now called the Standing Boy Flint Industry. Experts date the site back to at least 7,500-6,500 B.C., and point out that similar tool assemblages have been found further down the Chattahoochee in Houston County, Alabama, at the Stanfield-Worley shelter cave in northwest Alabama, to the east near Macon, Georgia, and at various other sites in the Southeast.

The Standing Boy site appears to have been the location of a tool industry, involving quartz as well as flint, for many hundreds of years, and may, in fact, have its roots in the preceding Paleo Period. Interestingly, much of the flint used at the Standing Boy site came from the Flint River. Apparently it was acquired in a crudely flaked form and then was finished locally.

As the fauna and flora of the Valley changed, the Indians of the Archaic Period had to adapt and learn new hunting and food-gathering techniques. The old heavy spears with their large Clovis points were not suitable for hunting deer and wild turkey. Lighter spears tipped with smaller, side-notched points proved more effective and easier to handle. In time, the people of the Valley became extremely

Atlatl with banner stone

skilled at throwing these lighter weapons. Around 5,000 B.C., they developed a spear-throwing device, called an atlatl, which hooked into a depression on the rear of the spear and enabled the thrower to hurl the weapon with great force. Sometimes they added a stone, called a banner stone by archaeologists, to the shaft of the atlatl. Although their precise purpose is still debated, banner stones may have slipped up and down the atlatl shaft, functioning as a sliding weight to increase the speed, and thus the penetrating power, of the spear. Banner stones were made in a variety of shapes, and many of them were beautifully finished and polished. They have been found throughout the Chattahoochee River Valley and in many other places in Georgia and Alabama.

Beginning of the Wilderness School

In addition to hunting, the Archaic Indians practiced extensive, systematic gathering of wild plant foods--nuts, berries, roots, and fruits--to supplement their meat diet. Thus it was that the Indians of the Archaic Period, who lived a more settled life than their Paleo ancestors, really began the painstakingly slow accumulation of knowledge of the local environment which made a better daily life possible for succeeding generations of Valley inhabitants. The accumulation of this knowledge, sometimes referred to as "primary forest efficiency," did not come quickly or easily. Even the acquisition of the most basic know-how required years, perhaps centuries. However, in a society so dependent upon hunting and gathering, mastery of the local environment was absolutely essential to survival. Animal habits had to be learned in the smallest detail. Edible plants, nuts, fruits, and roots had to be identified. The cataloging of medicinal plants and the uses of those which could provide material for home industry was begun. Trial and error must have been the only method, and it was not without its dangers. Some plants, such as jimson weed (*Datura stramonium*), were poisonous all the time. Some, such as pokeweed (*Phytolacca americana*), could be eaten only when young. Some nuts, including hickory nuts, walnuts, and chestnuts, could be eaten directly after they fell. Others, such as certain oak acorns, had to be leached to remove the bitter tannin, a laborious task that required the Indians to crack the nuts, place them in a sandy depression, and pour hot water over them again and again until they were palatable.

Thus began the education of the early Valley people in what we might call the Wilderness School, a necessary process of learning specifically oriented toward mastery of the local environment. Boys and girls began their education in this school when they were very young and continued in it for the rest of their lives. Its curriculum consisted of the geography, climatology, botany, and zoology of the Chattahoochee River Valley, plus practical and vital information on such topics as how to hunt, clean and prepare game, build a fire, treat snakebites or wounds, cure animal hides, fashion weapons, and find their way in the deep woods. In time, this Wilderness School became increasingly formalized, very nearly as much so as an American high school or vocational school. Apt students might apply to councils of "learned men" or apprentice themselves to a particular individual for further study. Eventually, if they worked hard enough and had the ability, a few of the students became learned men themselves, what the historical Indians of the Valley called "healers" or "knowers" and what we might today call historians, herbalists, psychologists, physicians, or worldly philosophers.

Importance of Nut-Bearing Trees

Among the first steps in mastering the wilderness was learning to identify and efficiently exploit the acorn- and nut-bearing trees in the Valley. It is difficult for us today to appreciate how important acorns and nuts were to the early inhabitants of the Valley. It may be true, for example, that the presence of large stands of oaks, hickories, and other nut-bearing trees was as important as the availability of game in attracting wandering bands of people to the Valley. Most likely, both exerted a strong attraction to a people who were dependent upon hunting and gathering for survival. Nuts are highly caloric and they provided much-needed fatty acids and protein in the diet of Archaic people. As stated, many acorns had to be leached of tannin before they were palatable, but they too were rich in protein and fats.

Among the most important nut-bearing trees of the Valley today are the hickories, including shagbark (*Carya ovata*), mockernut (*Carya tomentosa*), and pecan (*Carya illinoensis*); black walnut (*Juglans nigra*); chinquapin (*Castanea pumila*); and the hazelnuts (*Corylus spp.*). The American beech (*Fagus grandifolia*) was formerly present in the Valley in considerable numbers, but has been thinned out by clear-cutting, selective timbering, and ground clearing for farming. The chestnut (*Castanea dentata*) was also an important nut-bearing tree, especially around the Fall Line and in the lower Piedmont, but chestnut blight has killed off all the large chestnut trees in the Valley.

Although there is still some debate over whether the pecan is native to our area, all the above species are thought to have been present in the Valley by Archaic times, certainly by the late Archaic, and all bear sweet nuts that can be eaten raw as well as roasted out of the shell, which is probably how the Archaic people consumed them. It is not known if the Archaic people utilized the bitternut hickory (*Carya cordiformis*), which grows on the lower Chattahoochee and which would have required considerable treatment to make its nutmeat palatable to humans.

Among the many important oaks in the Valley we can list the white oak (*Quercus alba*), swamp chestnut oak (*Q. michauxii*), blackjack oak (*Q. marilandica*), live oak (*Q. virginiana*), black oak (*Q. velutina*), water oak (*Q. nigra*), sand laurel oak (*Q. hemisphaerica*), swamp laurel oak (*Q. laurifolia*), southern red oak (*Q. falcata*), Arkansas oak (*Q. arkansana*), northern red oak (*Q. rubra*), scarlet oak (*Q. coccinea*), turkey oak (*Q. laevis*), willow oak (*Q. phellos*), chestnut or rock chestnut oak (*Q. prinoides*), and post oak (*Q. stellata*).

A number of other species grow in our area, but these are among the most widespread. All are thought to have been present in the Valley since at least late Archaic times. Formerly, before American settlers cleared the bottomlands for agriculture and timbered the coves and hillsides above the tributaries of the river, the Valley was covered with oak trees and many other species of hardwoods. Once they reach maturity, which usually requires 20 years or more, most of the oaks furnish a crop of acorns at least every two to three years. The sweet acorns were naturally the favorites among the early inhabitants of the Chattahoochee River Valley, who quickly learned that the acorns from trees with leaves that were bristle-tipped or had jagged edges--the subgenus *Erythrobalanus* or red oaks--were apt to be bitter, whereas those from trees whose leaves were smooth and rounded--*Lepidoobalanus* or white oaks--were usually sweet. In our area, oaks that produced sweet acorns included the swamp chestnut oak, the lowly blackjack oak, the live oak, post oak, overcup oak (*Q. lyrata*), and white oak.

Actually, any oak acorn could be rendered palatable, and it should be noted that the common water oak is a red oak species that abounds in the Valley and produces a good crop of acorns. So do the laurel oaks and several other species.

Acorns were available from September through November in most of the Valley. October was the prime month for hickory nuts and walnuts.

Seasons

Gradually, over a period of many hundreds of years, as the people of the Valley began to master their environment, they congregated in larger groups and stayed in one place for longer stretches of time. In the spring and summer they would gather by the river and its tributaries to feast on freshwater clams and mussels, to eat fish--the first bone fishhooks found in Alabama date to the early Archaic--and to do what we would today call socializing. Summer was also the time when roots were dug and berries and wild fruits were harvested. Fall and winter were the seasons for gathering nuts and acorns near the Fall Line and in the hills above the flood plain throughout the Valley. The white-tailed deer (*Odocoileus virginianus*), which had become the primary game animal in the Valley by the seventh millennium B.C., was hunted throughout the year although the people would have noticed that deer were heaviest after fattening on the fall crop of acorns and nuts. The people's diet became more varied and nutritious and included more plants, roots, and wild fruits than Paleo Indians consumed.

However, the daily life of the people of the Valley was still extremely harsh by today's standards. Having no pottery and thus few vessels in which to prepare food, the women sometimes cooked in skin-lined pits filled with water. Rocks, heated in fires, were dropped into the water, quickly bringing it to a boil.

The hot rock technique may also have been used to cook food in crude bowls carved out of wood or sandstone. However, neither the wooden nor the sandstone bowls could be placed directly over flames. The wooden bowls would burn and the sandstone bowls would crack. Freshwater clams and mussels were also cooked with hot rocks, only in this instance many fist-sized rocks would be heated in a hardwood fire, then the ashes raked away, and the mussels, dripping with river water, placed on the rocks. The steam would quickly cook the shellfish.

Fortunate women possessed heat-resistant soapstone bowls made from steatite rock. Soapstone is soft, easily carved, and will not crack when exposed to direct heat. Although it is in limited supply in the lower Valley, extensive deposits are found in both the Georgia and Alabama Piedmonts. The closest prehistoric steatite quarries to the Valley were in the Hillabee schist deposits in the East Alabama Piedmont. The Archaic Indians of the Chattahoochee River Valley undoubtedly traded for raw steatite or for finished vessels with the inhabitants of the Piedmont.

Toward the middle of the Archaic Period, at around 4,000 B.C. when the Valley climate was beginning to stabilize, the Indians developed grooved stone axes and adzes, heavy tools that may have been used to fell trees to clear openings in the forest or perhaps to hollow out trees to make dugout canoes. We are not certain why the Archaic people wanted to clear fields. It may have had to do with attracting white-tailed deer, who prefer to feed on tender plant shoots on the fringes of open spaces. Perhaps the Archaic people had noticed that wild plants, including edible and medicinal plants, grow best when sunlight can reach them in the open.

Not surprisingly, given their dependence on acorns and nuts, the Archaic Indians also began to use grinding and nutting stones to crack and pound nuts. Numbers of nutting stones, some dating back to the Archaic, have been found in the Valley. They were made by chipping out shallow depressions in a flat rock. The depressions would hold nuts or acorns while they were cracked with a hammer stone. The nuts were then transferred to the grinding stone, which had a deeper and larger depression, where they were worked with a stone pestle to make a sort of meal or flour. Historic Indians in the Valley used the nut and acorn meal to thicken their stews and to make a dense, heavy bread. The Archaic Indians may have done the same.

White-Tailed Deer

However, as important as nuts and acorns were in the diet of Archaic people in the Valley, the essential element was the white-tailed deer, a valuable source of food, clothing, tools, and more. About half of a deer could be eaten; the rest was used in home manufacture. Its antlers and bones were fashioned into needles, fishhooks, spear points, awls and drills, flakers, pins, saws, scrapers, hammers, and ornaments. The animal's hide was fleshed, de-haired, and cured to be made into moccasins, containers, and clothing. The sinews and gut could be cured and made into thongs and twining. The heads of bucks were dried and, along with the cured hide, were probably worn by hunters when stalking wild deer or as headdresses on ceremonial occasions.

Deer, and indeed, all game animals were taken year-round. It was only thousands of years later, after contact with whites and the establishment of the European deer hide trade, that the Indians of the Valley began their massive fall and winter hunts. In a subsistence economy, no one could afford to pass up meat when it was available.

As the people's diet improved, they

began to live longer. The population of the Valley increased. Semi-permanent settlements were established at favorite locales, especially for spring and summer encampments. Hunting areas became more restricted as bands staked out their territories. Though

still minimal, creature comforts improved. Skin huts were replaced by more comfortable dwellings made from saplings driven into the ground and sided with interlaced sticks or mats of tree bark. The women wove baskets from split river cane or leathery strips of hickory or oak bark. They had also probably learned to make clothing from pounded tree bark or plant fibers. Their homes were floored with woven mats of split cane or vegetable fiber.

Although no Archaic burials have been found in the Valley proper--the soil in the Valley is so acidic it rapidly dissolves skeletal remains--they have been discovered nearby in Georgia, Florida, and Alabama. One of the oldest known burials in our region is that of an infant in a pit in Russell Cave in Jackson County, Alabama. It dates from around 6,500-6,200 B.C. Most of these ancient burials were in round holes dug in the earth. Usually, the bodies were flexed into fetal or sitting position prior to interment. A number of the Archaic burials in Alabama contain mortuary goods, among them soapstone bowls, presumably because they were highly valued personal possessions.

Middle Prehistoric
1,000 B.C. - A.D. 700

Formerly, men and animals talked to one another, and later they lost the ability to do so, but the great medicine men had the gift.

One time an old woman was much frightened at the sight of a yearling bull coming toward her bellowing, and she tried to escape. The bull reassured her, however, in language she could understand, saying, "Don't be afraid of me. I am just enjoying myself singing." He added that she must not tell of her experience or she would die.

After that the old woman knew the language of the animals and listened to them as they talked together.

She was blind in one eye, and once when she was shelling corn she heard the chickens say to one another, "Get around on her blind side and steal some of the corn." She was so much tickled at this that she laughed out loud.

Just then her husband, who was a very jealous man, came in and believed she must be thinking of some other man, so he said, "Why do you get so happy all by yourself?" Then she related her adventure with the bull and told him what the chickens had just been saying, but the moment she finished her story she fell over dead.

A Creek Tale

III

Woodland Period
1,000 B.C. - A.D. 700

Pottery

It was not until some time after 3,000 B.C. that the people of the Valley discovered how to make pottery by fire-tempering clay. Although it cannot be said with certainty, Valley Indians probably learned to make pottery from people living on the Georgia coast, either directly or through the process of cultural diffusion or trade. The oldest pottery yet found in North America is from the Stallings Island culture on the Savannah River near the Georgia coast. It dates from around 2,500 B.C. However, the shattered remnants of early clay vessels, called potsherds by archaeologists, can be found throughout the Southeast, including the Chattahoochee River Valley.

To make pottery, a little water and plant fiber were added to a lump of clay, which was worked by hand into a consistent mass. Initially, in the production of fiber-tempered pottery, the Indians seem to have simply formed this mass into a bowl or cup.

Pots were built up from coils of clay.

In time, however, they learned to add other strengthening agents--sand, grit, crushed mussel shells, even the crushed remains of old pots--and to roll the mixture out between their palms into narrow strips. These strips were coiled on top of each other, usually on a basal disc of the same mixture, until the desired size and shape was attained. A rock or piece of wood was then used to smooth the sides of the vessel, which was set aside to dry in the sun. Sometimes, at this stage, the Indians would incise or stamp a decorative design on the vessel. When it had dried and hardened in the sun, it was placed in a hot fire and baked for several hours. The finished pot was durable and would not crack or split when exposed to direct heat.

As simple as this process may seem today, pottery-making, ordinarily done by women, represented a tremendous step forward, both in domestic comfort and nutrition. The Valley Indians were now able to fry and boil food easily, prepare nutritious soups and stews, and more easily transport water and store food reserves for future use. Daily life, especially household chores, became much easier after the technique of making ceramic pottery became widely known.

For example, the once awkward and time-consuming process of leaching acorns in a sandy depression to remove the bitterness was made much simpler. Now all the Indians had to do was boil the acorns in a pot of water and periodically pour off and renew the water until all traces of bitterness had disappeared. The oil from walnuts and hickories could easily be extracted by crushing the nuts, shell and all, and boiling them in water. During this process, the shells would settle to the bottom, the nutmeats tended to float in suspension, and the oil rose to the top where it could be easily skimmed off. In historic times, oil of hickory nuts was a great favorite among the Indians of the Valley (and among white traders and settlers as well), who added it to stews and bread and used it extensively in almost all their cooking. The development of pottery probably greatly increased the Valley Indians utilization of nuts and acorns.

Archaeologists usually cite the discovery of pottery-making as an indicator of yet another line between time periods, this one separating the Archaic Period from the Woodland Period. The Woodland, one of the classic time divisions used in North American archaeology, lasts until about 700 A.D. It includes a local variation in our area known as the Gulf Formational

Period. However, all such titles are little more than convenient labels, and the dates that go with them are, at best, approximate. They are less important for our purposes than the changes taking place in the daily life of the people of the Valley. The development of the bow and arrow also took place at this time. The bow and arrow was a great advance over the spear, both for hunting and in war. It had a tremendous impact on the people's lives. They were now able to kill game, particularly deer, much more easily and in much greater numbers than ever before.

But perhaps the most significant development during this time was the gradual increase in wilderness knowledge, particularly in regards to knowledge of local plants and animals, that enriched the diet of the people of Valley and enabled them to live a more settled life. Often overlooked in the wealth of archaeological remains from this period, mastery of the local environment greatly improved the standard of living. It meant the people could stay in one place for longer periods. Although they still moved about a great deal, during the Woodland Period their favorite campsites became year-round residences--villages. More efficient exploitation of forest resources made a more settled life possible.

During this same period, bands became larger through marriage and childbirth. People probably lived longer due to better nutrition and a less strenuous life. More children reached maturity, at which time they took mates from other bands and produced more offspring. In this fashion, over the course of many years, bands grew from a few dozen to several hundred persons, finally reaching the stage where they might more properly be called tribes.

Tribal Life

Tribes gathered for seasonal celebrations and ceremonies, to exchange domestic goods, to arrange marriages, and perhaps to mourn the death of powerful leaders. They spoke the same language and had the same general cultural and spiritual beliefs.

Each tribe developed its own oral inventory of tribal history, origin tales, myths, and folk stories. They had their favorite campsites on the river and its tributaries and in the rolling hills of the uplands where the best hunting lands were located. The women of a given tribe began to return year after year to the same stands of oaks, hickories, walnuts, beeches, and chestnuts that produced the most nuts and acorns. As the population of the Valley tribes increased, they became more and more dependent on the game and wild nuts and fruits from these favorite hunting and food-gathering areas. In this manner, tribes became more territorial as the centuries passed and less inclined to tolerate intrusions onto their traditional lands by other bands or tribes.

The people also became more fixed in their seasonal occupations: Fall was the time to gather hardwood mast--acorns, hickory nuts, chestnuts, and walnuts.   In the winter, the men hunted and trapped, although as stated, game was taken whenever and wherever possible. Spring was the time when the largest and choicest seeds of wild food plants were planted. The succulent young leaves and flowers of many wild food plants were also harvested at this time; others reached maturity later in the summer. In time, corn, planted in the early spring and harvested in late July or August, would replace many wild plants in the human food chain. In summer, the people went to the falls where Columbus and Phenix City now stand and caught fish for their villages. Both men and women gathered mussels from the sandbars exposed as the water level dropped during the hot months.

Thus the great seasonal round, largely determined by the climate and physical features of the Valley and the Southeast, was firmly established. It would vary but little for hundreds of years--until the first Europeans began to arrive in the Valley in the early 17th century.

Trade

Through intermarriage and extended clan relationships, the Woodland people maintained contact with each other over a wide area. Trade or barter was a natural byproduct of such social contact. Indeed, the unequal distribution of raw materials and the increase in population during the Woodland Period probably made some degree of trade necessary. The bulk of such exchange was in raw materials and domestic articles, much of which was perishable and thus has limited or no archaeological visibility. Among such raw materials and manufactured articles were pottery clay and finished pots; many different kinds of wood or vegetable products, such as river cane for arrows, black locust for bows, hickory and oak for tool shafts; various plants, seeds and, in particular, medicinal herbs; hickory nut oil and bear oil (the latter was favored for frying and anointing the hair); split cane, white oak and hickory strips, and baskets and mats made from such materials; and wooden spoons and bowls. Flint, both in raw bulk and as finished projectile points, knives, scrapers and other tools, found a ready market. Cosmetic articles included the feathers of birds, shell and ceramic beads, red ochre and other pigments, freshwater pearls, shark and bear teeth, and exotic animal skins. Bear pelts, used for bedding, were also items of exchange. Food items included dried and smoked meat and fish, seed and root flour, dried fruits--particularly persimmons--suet cakes, and wild spices and herbs.

Although the majority of trade was done with neighboring tribes and villages, we know from artifacts recovered from sites of Indian settlements in and around the Valley that, from the Woodland period on, there was considerable trade between Valley Indians and people living in distant regions, including the Gulf Coast, in lower and upper Alabama, along the Flint River in Georgia, in the Appalachian region of what is now Georgia,

North Carolina and Tennessee, and as far away as Ohio and the Mississippi Valley. Much of this trade was in exotic materials often found in association with burials of high-status individuals, but some of it was in more ordinary items. Among the items Valley Indians obtained through trade from other inhabitants of the Southeast were marine shells, salt, and various plants from the Gulf Coast; salt, quartz, and other minerals from the Clarke County region of South Alabama; greenstone and steatite from the Alabama and Georgia Piedmont; and copper, mica, and possibly crystals from the Appalachians. The Flint River, as previously mentioned, produced a much-favored form of flint. More copper came into the Valley from East Tennessee and the Great Lakes region. Obsidian for making fine projectile points probably reached the Valley from the Rocky Mountains.

Trading trails spread throughout the Valley and beyond, reaching such distant regions as the Ohio and Mississippi River Valleys, and both the Atlantic and Gulf coasts. These trails often followed some natural feature, such as a river, stream, or open ridge. Water courses were particularly important. Trails, following tributaries, linked adjacent river systems and served as paths through the wilderness. In many instances, the heads of tributaries or creeks from one river system almost touched the heads of the tributaries of another river system, requiring only a short walk between the two.   Thus the Chattahoochee-Apalachicola river system was linked with the Alabama-Coosa-Tallapoosa, Ocmulgee, Flint, and others. Traveling upstream, the traders walked. Traveling down, they probably used dugout canoes or stretched animal hides over wooden frames fashioned on the spot and floated downstream.

Within the Valley itself, the most important and frequently used long trails would have been those that went up and down both banks of the Chattahoochee, linking villages and leading north to the mountains and south to Northwest Florida and the Gulf coast. These river trails were used in historic times by both Indians and Europeans, and traces of them may be found today. Usually, the river trails ran inland several hundred yards or even

Valley Indians traded with other tribes throughout the Southeast and beyond.

several miles from the river itself, crossing creeks where they were narrower and more fordable and avoiding the numerous swamps and canebrakes near the river's edge.

Ideas accompanied trade goods on the long foot paths winding through the wilderness, so that Indian tribes living in the Chattahoochee River Valley both influenced and were influenced by other tribes living hundreds of miles away. Indian traders from the Valley tribes roamed Eastern and Mid-western America, accumulating a thorough knowledge of its geography and topography. Centuries before the first European traders set foot in the New World, there was a class of traders living in the Valley whose traditions went back hundreds, even thousands, of years.

*The old-time beings were gathered together. They
began acting in different ways and showing different
qualities. Master-of-Breath observed them. Some
began jumping upon trees and running about.
Someone asked, "What sort of beings are those?"
"They are like panthers," someone answered.
"Henceforth they shall go about as panthers," said
Master-of-Breath. Then again, some began leaping
and running. "What are they like?" someone asked.
"Like deer," it was said. "Henceforth they shall go
about as deer," said Master-of-Breath. Then again,
some went hopping high among the leaves of trees and
alighted on the branches. "What are they like?" asked
somebody. "Like birds," someone answered. "They
shall be birds," said Master-of-Breath. Then again,
some were very fat and when they walked they made a
great noise on the ground. "What are they like?"
asked someone. "Like bears," was the answer. "They
shall be bears, then," said Master-of-Breath. Then
again, one started off to run but could not go fast.
When he came back he had black stripes near his eyes.
"What will that be?" (it) was asked. "It is like a
raccoon," said one. "That kind shall be raccoons,"
said Master-of-Breath. Then one was so fat and
round-bodied that when he started off he could hardly
walk. "What is that kind?" (it) was asked. "It is like a
beaver," someone answered. "They shall be the
beavers," said Master-of-Breath. Then again, one
kind was fat and could not run very fast. When this
one had gone off to a distance and returned, someone
asked, "What is that like?" "Like a mink." "They
shall go about as minks," said Master-of-Breath.
Then again, one was very swift when he started to run.*

He darted back and forth very quickly. "What is he like?" was the question. "Like a fox," came the answer. "That kind shall be foxes," said Master-of-Breath. Then again, one was very strong and could pull up saplings by the roots. He went off to a distance and returned. Then someone asked, "What is he like?" "Like the wind," was the answer. "That kind shall be wind," said Master-of-Breath. Then again, one started off into the mud. When he had come back out of it, someone asked, "What is he like?" "Like a mud-potato," it was answered. "Such shall be mud-potatoes," said Master-of-Breath. Then again, one of them had short legs,and his back was covered with ridges. When he started out and returned, someone asked, "What is he like?" "Like an alligator," was the answer. "That kind shall be alligators," said Master-of-Breath. Then again, one with stripes on his back went running off, and when he came back, someone asked, "What is he like?" "Like a skunk," was the answer. "That kind shall be skunks," said Master-of-Breath. Then again, one went away jumping, and when he came back to the starting place, someone asked, "What is he like?" "Like a rabbit," was the answer. "That kind shall be rabbits," said Master-of-Breath. Then again, one went off squirming along on the ground. When he returned, someone asked, "What is he like?" "Like a snake," was the answer. "That kind shall be snakes," said Master-of-Breath.

Master-of-Breath, after he had given them their forms on the earth, told them not to marry their own kind, but to marry people of other clans. All the red people know what clans they belong to and do not marry in their own clan. If they did they would not increase.

A Creek Tale

IV

Burial Mound Tradition

Clay platform pipe from Mandeville

As their standard of living increased, the people of the Valley had more time to think of matters beyond the daily struggle for survival. Spiritual matters and the question of what lay beyond the grave began to receive more attention. The early inhabitants of the Valley had probably always had a rich spiritual life, but we have little way of discovering what that spiritual life consisted of. We do know that some time after 1,000 B.C., Valley Indians came under the influence of a culture that placed special emphasis on burial of the dead. This new culture, which included elaborate funereal ceremonialism, may have come into North America from Mexico or Central America, and into the Southeast by way of the Midwest. It is not clear, however, whether the burial mound tradition was brought into the Southeast by a new wave of migrants or whether the local Indian

36

population was simply influenced by a more powerful and dynamic culture to the northwest.

Burial mounds are an Asiatic and Old World trait, and some experts think the American Indians, including those who lived in the Southeast and in the Chattahoochee River Valley, were influenced from those distant places. However, enormous blank spots across Canada and Eastern Asia where no mounds appear throw this interpretation into question. The most reasonable assumption, say many archaeologists and anthropologists, is that North American Indians, including those who lived in the Chattahoochee River Valley, were influenced by burial mound customs of the natives of both Middle and South America. Most specialists agree that farming, the beginnings of which appear in this period, was an import from Middle America. And many experts think the technique of pottery making came from the Colombian coast of South America. It may be that other cultural traits, including mound burials and the construction of earthworks and even effigy mounds such as those found at Poverty Point in the the lower Mississippi Valley, were passed on to the American Indians at the same time and came to fruition during this period.

Burial mounds were man-made tumuli of earth heaped over the dead, who were often buried with elaborate ceremony. The nature of the burials indicates the existence of some sort of systematized spiritual life and perhaps even the presence of an elite, priestly class. The size and construction of the mounds, which often contain tons of earth and other debris, indicates that the Valley Indians of this period had an advanced degree of social organization in their daily life. The mounds required thousands of hours to erect. They simply could not have been built without the cooperative efforts of numerous individuals.

The largest and most numerous of these mounds in the United States are found in the Ohio Valley, where they are associated with the Adena and Hopewell cultures, particularly the latter, and along the Mississippi River. However, there are many burial mounds dating from the Woodland Period in the

Tennessee Valley region of north Alabama and in the Chattahoochee River Valley. For example, the Mandeville site, located near the Georgia bank of the Chattahoochee near Fort Gaines, is--or was--one of the best-known burial mound sites in the Southeast. Now covered by the waters of Lake Walter F. George, the Mandeville site is believed to have dated from shortly before the birth of Christ. The huge Kolomoki complex near Blakely is another burial mound site, although its largest mound may date to a later period.

Mandeville

The Mandeville site consisted of two mounds, only one of which was a burial mound. Excavations carried out there in the late 1950s and early 1960s showed conclusively that the Woodland Indians of the lower Chattahoochee River Valley already had an elaborate culture and a complex social order, and that trade and possibly religious affiliations existed between the people of the Valley and those in Ohio, Illinois, north Alabama and north Georgia, and in the Gulf Coast area of Florida.

The two mounds at Mandeville were on a bluff above Sandy Creek. Between the mounds, which were approximately 900 feet apart, was a wide triangular area believed to have been a village site. Mound A was a platform mound and apparently contained no burials. However, Mound B was clearly identified as a burial mound. Objects recovered from the mound and its immediate vicinity include burned fragments of human bones, indicating cremation, a clay female figurine three-and-a-half inches high, several so-called "pan pipes" of river cane covered by copper (and in one instance, silver foil), more than a dozen copper ear spools and numerous other objects of copper, a clay platform pipe, lumps of galena, and nearly a dozen ground greenstone celts.

Mound A, the platform mound, appears to have been repeatedly rebuilt or resurfaced by successive generations of inhabitants of the area. It yielded from its lowest and hence oldest stratum a human figurine head and two clay female torso fragments, part of a platform pipe that had a bird effigy bowl, several flaked flint knives, fragments of copper, graphite, several quartz crystals, and quantities of mica.

Copena and Hopewell Cultures

The Mandeville site is particularly intriguing because most of the artifacts listed above are securely identified with the Copena culture of North Alabama and the Tennessee Valley or with the widespread and influential Hopewell culture of Ohio and Illinois. The Copena culture, so-called because of the copper and galena found at Copena sites, flourished between A.D. 100 and 500. It is characterized by burial in caves as well as mounds. The Hopewell Culture, which was much larger and more influential than Copena, is usually dated from around 400 B.C. to A.D. 400. It was one of the great prehistoric cultures in North America.

Centered in the Ohio Valley, particularly along the Scioto River, the Hopewell people erected huge burial mounds and effigy earthworks. They also were sophisticated craftsmen and artists whose products are among the most beautiful and intriguing of all Indian art. Many of these products were interred in the burial mounds along with human skeletons or cremated human remains. Grave goods associated with the Hopewell Culture include clay figurines, pan pipes wrapped in copper or silver, platform tobacco pipes, copper earspools, gorgets, bracelets, beads, and other objects.

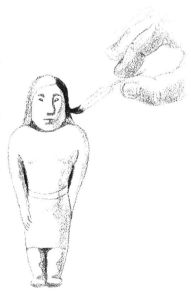

Copper ear spools

Among the latter are copper falcons, fish, a helmet inlaid with pearls and mica, and an elaborate and highly stylized serpent head. Mica from North Carolina was fashioned into intricate designs by Hopewell artisans, and some graves were lined with mica. The dead were also buried in pits lined with logs, bark, or clay and were then covered with several layers of earth. Most were burned or subjected to some sort of ritual firing before being covered with earth.

The Hopewell Culture, which apparently included a rich imaginative life and a complex system of beliefs about the spirit world, spread throughout the Midwest and as far west as Oklahoma and south into Georgia and Alabama. The Mandeville mounds are clear evidence that this culture reached the lower Chattahoochee River Valley some time around the birth of Christ.

Unfortunately, the burial mound at Mandeville had been considerably disturbed before archaeologists excavated it, making it a difficult site to interpret. Many of its artifacts may have been taken by pot hunters and sold to private collectors. However, the mounds at Kolomoki, which are representative of what archaeologists call the Gulf Coast tradition, survived the centuries more or less intact. They offer an excellent example of the elaborate ritual with which the Woodland Indians of the Valley buried their dead.

Kolomoki

There are nine mounds at the Kolomoki site, which covers 300 acres and is now a state park. It is located on Kolomoki Creek, about six miles from the Chattahoochee and a few miles north of the modern town of Blakely. Only two of the nine mounds at Kolomoki have definitely been identified as burial mounds. One of the other mounds is an enormous flat-topped heap of earth 56 feet high, 325 feet long, and 200 feet wide at its base. Archaeologist do not believe this is a burial mound. The two burial mounds are located west of the large flat-topped mound, and although they are much smaller, they reveal a great deal about the lives of the people who inhabited the site. A detailed look at how one of the mounds was constructed will serve as an example of burial mound practices.

First, the Kolomoki people cleared an area about 50 feet in diameter. Five bodies, with flexed knees and a few beads, were then covered in the earth in log-lined graves. While the dead were being buried, eight large logs were held in a vertical position. These poles were secured by earth from mounding over the graves and by other debris. The small mound over the five graves was then covered with rocks, leaving the eight poles or "scaffold" protruding above the mound.

After this, a single male was buried in a rock slab and log grave at the southern edge of the scaffold. Earth was then piled into and over this grave, and several individuals were cremated on top of the heap. Following this, a square framework, perhaps a litter, was placed over the cremated remains. In front of the scaffold, two women, the only females in the mounds, were placed in separate log and rock slab graves, side by side.

After these burials, the people of Kolomoki raised a five-foot platform mound over the dead, the scaffold still protruding above the pile. At the eastern edge of the mound, they then placed many pottery vessels, sherds, and human heads.

In the next stage, they buried and cremated in place a number of individuals and skulls as well as bone bundles. They threw rocks onto the cremations while the fire was still burning. Finally, the Kolomoki people piled more earth over the entire structure, making it into a flat-top mound. On the top, they cremated complete bodies, long human bones, and skulls. The entire conglomerate was then coated with from three to 10 feet of red clay that produced a dome-shaped burial mound 20 feet high and 100 feet in diameter.

Archaeologist William Sears, who excavated the site, thinks the bulk of the construction took place in a continuous operation, indicating a lengthy and highly ritualistic ceremony. He also believes that each burial mound was intended to be a monument to a single individual, namely the person in the main burial pit or area.

It is possible that a number of individuals were sacrificed on the death of the important person--one anthropologists calls such a leader a "Big Man," a more accurate description than "chief"-- for whom the tomb was intended. It may be that the two females in the mound represent a form of wife sacrifice, although this is highly speculative. At any rate, it seems unlikely that so many people died natural deaths simultaneously. Some form of retainer sacrifice would seem to be indicated.

Of course, it is possible that the people found cremated and buried in this stage of the mound did not die at the same time. Their bodies--or more likely, their bones--may have been preserved in a sort of mortuary until the death of the Big Man or some other event or factor occasioned their interment.

From other excavations at Kolomoki, it is known that the people lived in a fan-shaped area radiating outward from the enormous, flat-topped mound on the eastern edge of the complex. Estimates of the population at the time of greatest density during the Woodland Period range from 1,500 to 2,000 persons. Obviously, an elaborately constructed mound such as was found at the site could not have been built without a sizable population, a population that took part in a long and involved burial ceremony at the death of some important civic or religious leader.

This emphasis on burial has led some people to conclude that a cult of the dead existed during this period. Most anthropologists dislike the use of the word "cult" to describe what took place. The evidence is simply that the Indians buried some of their leaders or Big Men in mounds. We do not know whether these men were great warriors or administrative figures who achieved high status through native ability. They may even have been religious leaders, shamans, or "priests." Thus, even at this early date, we have the possibility of a stratified society. Perhaps the principal persons interred in the mounds were connected with trade. Both Mandeville and Kolomoki were ideally located to control the river trade route between the upper Piedmont and the Gulf Coast and the overland paths between tribes living on the Atlantic and those in what are now west Alabama and Mississippi. Some archaeologists believe the principal burials were connected with the new practice of agriculture, with the increasing dependence of the population on corn (maize) or other cultigens now essential to their diet. Such individuals may have had special responsibility to appease the gods so that the corn or other crops would flourish, the weather remain favorable, and a good harvest be made. It is possible that they were directly associated with the sun, whose influence on the plant world would have been obvious to the early people of the Valley. Fire, the sun's representative on earth, may also had figured in the Mandeville and Kolomoki peoples' spiritual beliefs. Certainly fire was an essential element in their elaborate burial ceremonialism. And the other natural elements--water, wind, lightning, thunder--bore directly on the peoples' daily life and were probably a part of their spiritual beliefs as well.

Since the mounds were built of earth laboriously transported, basketful by basketful, from borrow pits, anthropologists say we may assume some division or organization of labor, a sign that these early residents of the Valley could undertake and complete a civic project of some size. It has been estimated that Mound A at Kolomoki would have required approximately 875,000 man-hours to complete.

Woodland people not only built mounds, they also constructed stone enclosures and effigy mounds, such as the ceremonial enclosures atop Fort Mountain in north Georgia and the DeSoto Falls earthwork on the Little River in Alabama. The well-known eagle effigy mound in Eatonton, Georgia, dates from around 500 B.C. Remnants of a stone enclosure have been found in the

Chattahoochee River Valley atop Pine Mountain, and there are many curious piles of stones along the Chattahoochee on both banks. Although periodic flooding and extensive farming have all but obliterated the original configurations of these stones, archaeologists believe the Valley people of Woodland times participated in some sort of ritual or ceremonial activity inside stone enclosures or rings, a practice identified with the Hopewell culture or with the slightly earlier Adena culture, both centered in the Ohio River Valley.

Art

The mounds and ceremonial rings indicate other developments in the daily life of Valley Indians of the Woodland Period. Clearly, they now had sufficient leisure time to allow them to undertake civic projects not directly associated with food-gathering or with hunting. Along with civic projects we must list art, for as we have seen with the Hopewell Culture, many artifacts recovered from the Woodland Period had been handsomely fashioned and decorated far beyond anything required for mere utility. There are beautifully carved greenstone celts (almost as smooth as polished metal), polished atlatl weights or banner stones, effigy pipes skillfully moulded and carved, ceremonial projectile points or ceremonial blades that show the accumulated skill of centuries of experience working stone, and, of course, pottery, which the Woodland people had learned to temper or strengthen by adding sand or crushed rock to the clay.

In the Woodland Period, a particular type of pottery known as Swift Creek appears. Swift Creek ware is found throughout the Chattahoochee River Valley. It is distinctively decorated with whorling, geometric designs that often suggest Eastern mandalas. Its various motifs show a highly developed sense of line and form. This is a striking development. Such art--for that is what it is--requires not only leisure time but creative processes that lie beyond mere abstract reasoning and the development of new technologies. We do not normally think of prehistoric

Americans as capable of such creativity, but clearly they were.

Stone rings may have had ceremonial use.

It is said that corn was obtained by one of the women of the Tamalgi clan. She had a number of neighbors and friends, and when they came to her house she would dish some sofkee (a native dish made from corn) into an earthen bowl and they would drink it. They found it delicious, but did not know where she got the stuff of which to make it. Finally they noticed that she washed her feet in water and rubbed them, whereupon what came from her feet was corn. She said to them, "You may not like to eat from me in this way, so build a corncrib, put me inside and fasten the door. Don't disturb me, but keep me there for four days, and at the end of the fourth day you can let me out."

They did so, and while she was there they heard a great rumbling like distant thunder, but they did not know what it meant. On the fourth day they opened the door as directed and she came out. Then they found that the crib was well stocked with corn. There was corn for making bread, hard flint corn for making sofkee, and other kinds. She instructed them how to plant grains of corn from what she had produced. They did so, the corn grew and reproduced, and they have had corn ever since.

A Creek Tale

V

Wilderness School
Part One: Vegetable Kingdom

Although the emergence of the burial mound tradition usually receives most of the attention in archaeological and anthropological texts dealing with the Woodland Period, the most dominant factor in the daily lives of the people was still the struggle for existence. Their victory in this struggle may well represent their most significant achievement. During the Woodland Period, the people of the Chattahoochee River Valley became masters of the forest--skilled hunters and highly efficient gatherers of wild plants, nuts, and fruits. They were the last occupants of the Valley not dependent upon corn culture and subsistence agriculture, both of which began during the Woodland Period but did not reach full maturity until the subsequent Mississippian Period (A.D. 700-1,600).

The Woodland people roamed the Valley in search of game and wild plants, from which they got almost all their daily needs. Aided by the development of the bow and arrow, which became the weapon of choice during the Woodland Period, the Valley Indians became supremely accomplished hunters. Mastery of the forest and of the plants and creatures within it made them at home in the wilderness. As such, they probably came as close as any native Americans to the idealized concept most people have of what it means to be "Indian"--to exist in a state of nature entirely dependent upon wild game and plants for sustenance and upon one's wits and physical skills for survival and domestic comforts.

The Woodland people, and those who followed them, learned the Valley's topography by walking on it and immersing themselves in it. It was a knowledge imprinted on the heart as well as the mind. They waded its dark swamps in quest of bear and cougar, traversed its vast forests in search of stands of oaks, hickories, walnuts, and other nut-bearing trees, climbed its rugged hills--often for the same reason we do--to get a better view, and sank up to their waists in its shallow beaver ponds to collect cattails and bullhead lilies and dig up yellow pond lily roots with their toes. They knew the river itself, and its many tributaries, better than we know the streets on which we live. They swam and fished in its waters, used it as a broad highway to travel throughout the Valley, stretched out on its banks to take in the warmth of the winter sun, listened to the hiss of rain striking its surface, and heard the strange, sad, rustling sound of wind in the cane that grew on its banks.

In the daily struggle for survival, and in the simple fact of existence, the Woodland Indians became the greatest naturalists the Valley has ever known. They made use of almost everything and wasted nothing. There was scarcely an animal or a plant in the Valley that was not utilized by the Woodland people. Animals not only provided food, but their skins, bones and sinews were used to fashion useful articles, including clothing, bow strings, drills, hoes, tool handles, needles, and the like. Fish provided flesh for food. Their teeth, scales, and bones were made into arrowheads, cutting and puncturing tools, and articles of adornment. Wild plants which we consider to be weeds were a vital source of food, medicine, and raw material for domestic use and manufacture. Never before or since have the people of the Valley known so much about their surroundings--or turned them to such useful purpose--as during the Woodland Period.

Valley Cornucopia

The Chattahoochee River Valley was a horn-of-plenty during the Woodland Period. Even today, after centuries of destruction of its natural habitat, the area is as rich in wild life as many nature preserves. It is home to nearly 50 species of mammals, 250 kinds of birds, and more than 100 species of reptiles and amphibians. More than 100 kinds of fish can be found in its waters, which include, in addition to the river itself, large feeder creeks, beaver ponds and oxbows, and numerous small lakes. Many kinds of trees abound here, a combination of Piedmont and Coastal Plain species that includes pine, oak, hickory, sycamore, gum, locust, elm, dogwood, maple, cedar, sassafras, birch, beech, magnolia, yellow poplar, ash, cherry, willow, and persimmon. Natural groundcover includes weeds, grasses, vines, and shrubs, many of which are edible and nearly all of which can be put to some use.

Learning the characteristics and habits of the animals, and mastering the habitat identification and uses of wild plants, constituted a significant portion of any Indian's education before the coming of the white man. Along with this essential biological and ecological knowledge went woodcraft--how to build a fire, stay warm, erect a wilderness shelter, not get lost. It is this process we have chosen to call the "Wilderness School."

Sexual Roles
Historical Indians of the Valley--that is, those who were here after Europeans and Africans arrived--had distinct notions of the roles of the sexes in daily life, emphasizing a sharp division of labor and assigning the men and women quite different responsibilities. There is no reason to think it was any different among the Woodland people. In addition to the responsibility of defending the clan, village, or tribe against its enemies, men were expected to provide meat for the pot. As a consequence, they must have spent a good deal of their time making and maintaining their weapons, and perfecting their hunting techniques and knowledge of animal habits. Women bore and reared children, maintained the home, and were responsible for cleaning and cooking game and, especially, for gathering wild plants and nuts. As a result of the latter, women spent almost as much time in the woods as men, although their reasons for being there were quite different.

Boys began to handle spears, blowguns, and bows and arrows almost as soon as they could walk, and they were expected to bring home small game for the family pot whenever they could. Squirrels, rabbits and birds, often taken with a blowgun, were their first prey, and mastering the habits of these creatures prepared them for larger game. By their early teens, Indian boys were hunting turkey and deer, and many a Woodland youth would have been in on a bear kill long before his twentieth birthday.

Girls were put to work with domestic chores, learning to clean and prepare game for cooking. They also began to learn at an early age how to make pottery and clean and dress animal skins. Equally important, as soon as they were able, they accompanied their mothers and aunts and sisters on forages for wild foods, beginning at a very early age to learn to identify the habitats of useful plants and to build their own plant lists and locations. It has been estimated that early Indians of North America could identify several hundred plants by sight, so the learning process was necessarily rigorous and thorough. Men were involved in amassing knowledge about the vegetable kingdom also, especially in regards to the medicinal and ritual uses of plants.

Wild Plants

It would be impossible to list here all the plants from which the people of the Valley derived benefit during Woodland and later times, but perhaps we can get some idea by listing the most important ones and some of their uses. These plants can be broken down into three categories according to their use: food, domestic manufacture, and medicine.

The food plants were, of course, the most important. These, in turn, can be divided into several categories according to the parts favored and consumed by the Indians, as leaves and stems, flowers, fruit, seeds, nuts, or roots. Learning to identify specific food plants and to separate them into categories according to the parts that were edible would have been one of the first lessons in survival learned by all Woodland children, male or female. Other early lessons would have been on when and where to look for food plants, a function, respectively, of seasonal availability and habitat.

Leafy Plants

Perhaps the most readily utilized plants were those whose leaves and stems could be consumed raw or cooked, much as we might eat greens in a salad or prepare spinach, celery, or asparagus. Although loss of habitat has radically altered plant life in the Valley, obliterating many plant communities and significantly reducing the numbers of others, it is likely that any wild plant found in the Valley today that is not a clear introduction--honeysuckle, kudzu, dandelion, Cherokee rose, chickory--was present in Woodland times. Lamb's-quarters may have been introduced by Europeans, but other chenopods appear to have been present in the Valley in prehistoric times. In some instances, we have archaeological or paleontological evidence for the existence and use of certain plants, and there is ethnobotanical or historical documentation for the use of others.

Based on all these sources, and on modern-day checklists and personal observation, among the most important leafy plants available to Indians in the Chattahoochee River Valley during Woodland and later times were some form of the chenopods, possibly Lamb's-quarters (*Chenopodium album*), various greenbriars (*Smilax spp.*), pokeweed (*Phytolacca americana*), cattails (*Typha spp.*), pickerel weed (*Pontederia cordata*), water hyacinth (*Eichhornia crassipes*), shepherd's purse (*Capsella bursa-pastoris*), the peppergrasses (*Lepidium spp.*), water lilies (*Nymphaea spp.*), amaranths (*Amaranthus spp.*), curled or yellow dock (*Rumex crispus*), Solomon's-Seals (*Polygonatum spp.*), False Solomon's-Seal (*Smilacina racemosa*), bracken fern (*Pteridium aquilinum*), cheeses or common mallow (*Malva neglecta*), horseradish (*Armoracea lapathifolia*), so-called cut-leaved toothwort (*Dentaria laciniata*), purslane (*Portulaca oleracea*), yellow wood-sorrel *(Oxalis stricta)*, the chickweeds (*Stellaria* and *Cerastium spp.*), harbinger-of-spring (*Erigenia bulbosa*), common plantain (*Plantago major*), goosegrass

(*Galium aparine*), white sweet clover (*Melilotus alba*), wild clovers (*Trifolium spp.*), ox-eye daisy (*Chrysanthemum leucanthemum*), the wild mustards (*Brassica spp.*), wild parsnip (*Pastinaca sativa*), common evening-primrose (*Oenothera biennis*), Indian cucumber root (*Medeola virginiana*), the sow thistles (*Sonchus spp.*), wild lettuce (*Lactuca spp.*), water-shield lily (*Brassenia schreberi*), toadshade or sessile trillium (*Trillium sessile*), the wild onions, including wild garlic (*Allium spp.*), wood-nettle (*Laportea canadensis*), wild grapes (*Vitis spp.*), great bulrush (*Scripus spp.*), sheep sorrel (*Rumex acetosella*), lady's thumb and various smartgrasses (*Polygonum spp.*), bull thistle (*Cirsium vulgare*), dayflowers (*Commelina spp.*), waterleaf (*Hydrophyllum macrophyllum*), pilewort (*Erechtites hieracifolia*), galinsoga (*Galinsoga spp.*), American lotus (*Nelumbo lutea*), sweetflag (*Acorus calamus*), trout-lily (*Erythronium americanum*), sicklepod (*Cassia tora*), jewelweed (*Impatiens capensis*), such roses (*Rosa spp.*) as sweetbrier and pasture rose, and the blue and birdfoot violets (*Viola papilionacea* and *pedata*).

Most of these leafy plants were extremely nutritious. Green leaves contain large quantities of vitamin A as well as other vitamins, and such minerals as iron, copper, magnesium, and calcium. Leafy plants are best harvested in the spring, when the leaves and shoots are new and tender. Later in the year, many of the leaves become bitter and the stems tough. Some leaves, such as those of pokeweed, become poisonous at maturity.

Flowers

Although flowers were not a major food source, many plants and trees of the Valley produced flowers which are edible. Among these are the black locust tree (*Robinia pseudo-acacia*), wisteria (*Wisteria spp.*), elderberry (*Sambucus canadensis*), water-hyacinth (*Eichhornia crassipes*), violets (*Viola spp.*), redbud (*Cercis canadensis*), and wild mustard (*Brassica spp.*). Contemporary naturalists sometimes dip locust flowers in batter and fry them as fritters. In historic times, Indian women were

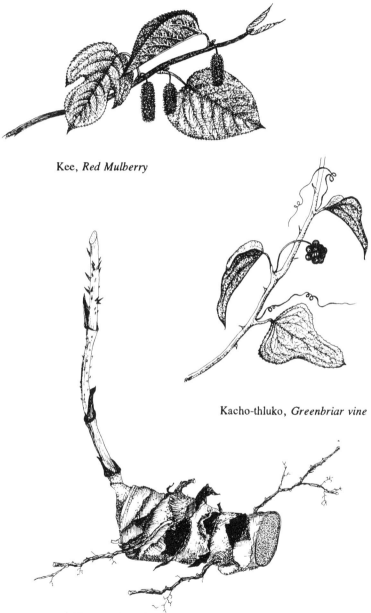

Kee, *Red Mulberry*

Kacho-thluko, *Greenbriar vine*

Kuntee, *Greenbriar root*

Osa, *Pokeweed*

Chetto Sewekeda, *Arrowhead*

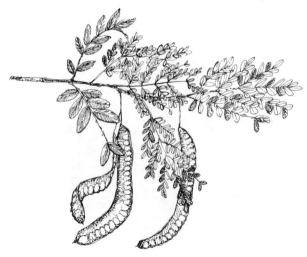

Katokwa, *Honey locust*

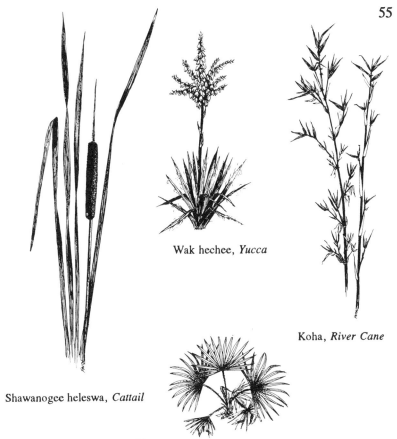

Wak hechee, *Yucca*

Koha, *River Cane*

Shawanogee heleswa, *Cattail*

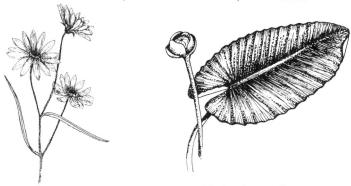

She-apo-entala *or* tala akshee, *Saw Palmetto*

Hasee-ahakee, *Sun Flower*

Weaktaphee, *Yellow Pond Lily*

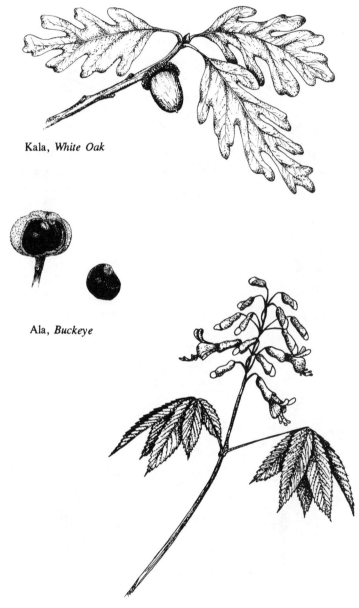

Kala, *White Oak*

Ala, *Buckeye*

Buckeye leaves and flowers

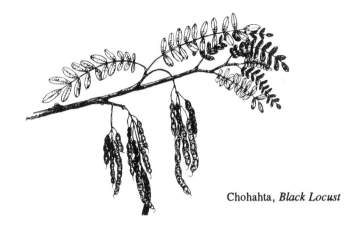

Chohahta, *Black Locust*

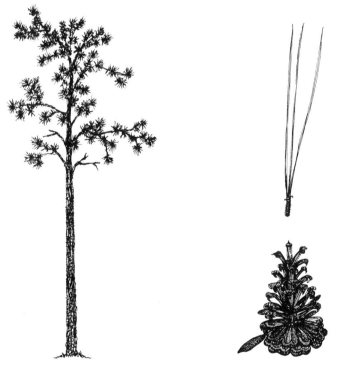

Chulee, *Long-leaf Pine*

Pine needles and cone

Aha-aklaukee, *Man-of-the-Earth*

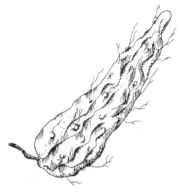

Root of Man-of-the-Earth

River Birch bark

Ak-chetolaska, *River Birch*

Tawa, *Staghorn Sumac*

Ahahwa, *Black Walnut*

Towaska, *Chestnut*

Ochee, *Shagbark Hickory*   Sat-ta, *Persimmon*

60

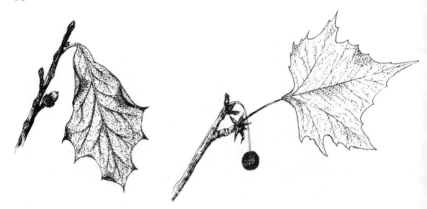

Secha, *Black-jack Oak*

Ak-hatka, *Sycamore*

Meskolwa, *Swamp Chestnut Oak*

Meskalwa, *Water Oak*

much more likely to put flowers in their hair than eat them.

Fruits

Wild fruits were more important than flowers in the diet of Valley Indians. Fruit was gathered in the late summer and early fall. Some of it was eaten straight from the bush or tree, but the Indians seem to have preferred to dry their fruit over a slow fire or in the sun. By preserving fruits in this manner, they would be available during the winter.

We have already remarked upon the fondness historic Indians of the Valley had for persimmons (*Diospyros virginiana*), which they ate ripe and which they sun-dried and baked into a heavy bread. Perhaps the second favorite fruit of the Indians was the red mulberry (*Morus rubra*), once quite popular among early European settlers in the Valley. Red mulberries ripen early--the historic Creek and Yuchi name for May was Moon of the Mulberry. Mulberries were eaten fresh or cooked. So were blackberries (*Rubus spp.*), serviceberries (*Amelanchier spp.*), elderberries (*Sambucus canadensis*), the May-apple (*Podophyllum peltatum*), wild strawberries (*Fragaria spp.*), partridgeberries (*Mitchella repens*), rose hips (*Rosa spp.*), juniper berries (*Juniperus spp.*), yucca or Spanish bayonet (*Yucca aloifolia*), pawpaw (*Asimina triloba*), hackberries (*Celtis occidentalis*), the aforementioned wild grapes (*Vitis spp.*)--especially the scuppernong (*Vitis rotundifolia*)--crabapples (*Pyrus spp.*), hawthorns (*Crataegus spp.*), wild plums (*Prunus spp.*), blueberries (*Vaccinium spp.*), and chokeberries (*Pyrus spp.*).

Although there is some question as to the presence of the passion-flower or maypop (*Passiflora incarnata*) in the Valley in Woodland times, it was here in abundance during the historic period. The Indians ate the pulpy fruit raw or baked it into a sort of bread.

Roots (Potatoes)

Many plants in the Valley produce tuberous roots, a vital source of starch and sugar for the Indians (and for early white traders and settlers as well). Some of these plants were among the most important of all wild foods. Chief among these were the greenbrier (*Smilax spp.*), called *kuntee* by the historic Creeks. Greenbrier can be found throughout the Chattahoochee River Valley. One species, the so-called bullbrier greenbrier (*Smilax bona-nox*), produces a very large root. Wild potato-vine (*Ipomoea pandurata*) was another extremely important Indian food. This is the white morning glory so common on roadsides in the Valley. It has a large rootstock that can weigh up to 20 pounds. Early white settlers called it wild sweet potato or man-of-the-earth, by which names it is still known in some rural sections. The highly nutritious tubers of the arrowhead (*Sagittaria spp.*), a common water plant in these parts, were dug by Indian women, as were the equally important root tubers of the yellow pond-lily (*Nuphar spp.*) and the water-shield (*Brasenia schreberi*). Other important root plants were wild carrot or Queen Anne's lace (*Daucus carota*), golden club (*Orontium aquaticum*), the Indian cucumber-root (*Medeola virginiana*), spurge-nettle (*Cnidoscolus stimulosus*), common evening-primrose (*Oenothera biennis*), groundnut (*Apios americana*), cattail (*Typha spp.*), arrow arum (*Peltandra virginica*), Virginian meadow-beauty (*Rhexia virginica*), great bulrush (*Scirpus spp.*), and probably American lotus (*Nelumbo lutea*).

Jerusalem artichoke (*Helianthus tuberosus*), which has a large, very palatable root, is widespread in the Chattahoochee River Valley today. Many botanists regard it as a Midwestern species and think it is a relatively recent introduction into our area. However, there is some evidence that historic Indians of the Valley knew the plant and ate it whenever they could.

Valley Indians harvested all of these wild potatoes whenever available, but they were particularly fond of tubers in the fall when they were full of starch and in the spring when they were very sweet with sugar. Sometimes the Indians ate them raw, but most were cooked over coals or boiled in several changes of water. Many roots--greenbrier, wild sweet potato, arrowhead--

were chopped or pounded and then reduced to flour by triculation or boiling, thus storing their food energy for later use.

Seeds and the Beginnings of Agriculture

Seeds were also important in the diet of Woodland Indians in the Valley. In fact, seeds remained important in the Indian diet right into historic times. The sunflower (*Helianthus spp.*) was probably the most important of these plants locally. The Creeks called it *hasee-ahakee*, "picture of the sun." In the fall, its nutritious seeds were collected in large quantities and eaten raw or parched. A sort of Indian pablum was made by mothers, who chewed sunflower seeds and fed the pulpy mass to infants. A fine oil was obtained by boiling the crushed kernels. The narrow-leaved sunflower (*Helianthus augustifolius*) is perhaps the most numerous of the sunflowers in the Valley today. The chenopods (*Chenopodium spp.*) are of considerable antiquity in the Valley. Their seeds were, and still are, widely eaten in the Eastern United States. Lamb's-quarters (*Chenopodium album*) is the most visible of these "goosefoots" today, but recent research suggests that another species (*C. berlindieri*) may have been cultivated by the Woodland Indians. Other seed-plants include the amaranths (*Amaranthus spp.*), large cane (*Arundinaria gigantea*), yellow pond-lilies (*Nuphar spp.*), wild mustard (*Brassica spp.*), the various clovers (*Trifolium spp.*), golden club (*Orontium aquaticum*), hog-peanut (*Amphicarpa bracteata*), pickerelweed (*Pontederia cordata*), great bulrush (*Scripus spp.*), purslane (*Portulaca oleracea*), wild bean (*Phaseolus polystachios*), and blue vervain (*Verbena hastata*).

Seeds were important for another reason. By husbanding and then planting the hardiest and largest of seeds from their favorite plants, Indian women may have given birth to domestic agriculture during Woodland times. Squash seeds (*Curcubita pepo*) were eaten by the Valley people perhaps as early as the second millennium B.C. when this hardy plant was introduced from what is now Mexico. Sunflowers appear to have been of particular importance in the beginning of seed culture, as were the aforementioned chenopods, knotweed (*Polygonum aviculare*), so-called little barley grass (*Hordeum pussillum*), the amaranths, smartweeds, an extinct form of sumpweed (*Iva annua*), giant ragweed (*Ambrosia trifida*), and maygrass (*Phalaris caroliniana*).

The food value of these plants would gradually have improved due to selection and the beginnings of cultivation, perhaps originally no more than the scattering of the better seeds in the rich soil of the river floodplain or the clearing away of other competitive plants. In time, the cultivated plants produced much larger and more nutritious seeds than in the common plant of the same type. The giant, commercially grown sunflowers of today show what can be achieved through selection and cultivation.

Nuts

We have already seen how important nuts were to Valley Indians. It is worth repeating, however, that nuts and acorns were an essential part of the Valley Indians' diet from at least the Archaic Period on. Both nuts and acorns were eaten raw and parched, added to stews and soups, and sometimes dried and ground into flour. Acorn bread was a common food among Indians throughout the Southeast. Hickory nuts yielded the sweetest of all Indian vegetable oils, but walnuts and beech nuts were also boiled to extract their oil. Nut oil was frequently used in soups and stews by Indians in the Valley. It was a standard ingredient in venison stew. However, nut oil was rarely used for frying because it becomes unstable under high heat. Sometimes women rubbed it into their hair. For daily use, it was kept handy in a squash gourd, and it stored well in large pots or skins in the ground. Of course, nut and acorn meat could be dried and stored. Valley Indians commonly stored acorns in pits dug in the earth, just as squirrels and chipmunks do. As long as they stayed cool, the acorns remained edible throughout the year.

Other Plant Food Sources

Many other wild plants, shrubs and trees provided foodstuff for Valley Indians. The saw palmetto (*Serenoa repens*) grows in profusion in the lower Chattahoochee River Valley. The terminal bud of saw palmetto contains the palm heart, one of the best-tasting of all wild foods. Flour could be made from the inner bark of a number of trees, including the slippery elm (*Ulmus ruba*) and from various pines (*Pinus spp.*). Bear-grass (*Yucca filamentosa*) supplied edible leaves and flowers. Cattail (*Typha spp.*), already mentioned under roots, was an incredibly versatile and valuable plant that furnished a variety of foods-- young shoots, stalk, flowers, pollen, sprouts, roots--and had many industrial uses as well.

Cattail Uses

In many ways, cattails almost constitute a Wilderness School in themselves. They were once found throughout the Valley, but destruction of habitat, particularly through the draining of beaver ponds and oxbows, has greatly reduced their numbers. As recently as the early 1800s, however, cattails were an essential ingredient in the daily lives of Valley Indians. The native people ate the tender shoots and stalks in the spring, either raw or cooked like asparagus. The immature flower spikes could also be boiled and eaten in late spring. Indian women gathered a nutritious pollen from the flower heads in early summer. The pollen could be used like flour. Late in the summer, sprouts appear on the rootstocks. They last all winter and are quite edible. In fall and winter, the roots of cattails are filled with starch. An excellent flour can be made by pounding and washing the roots until the starch settles out.

But that is not all. Cattails were also important in domestic manufacture. Their stalks could be made into mats, the down from the germinating flower heads was used for padding or as diapers for infants (as was Spanish moss), and the flowerheads made excellent torches.

Salt And Sugar

The Woodland Indians had many sources for both salt and sugar. Salt could be obtained through trade with coastal tribes or those that lived near inland salt licks or salt springs in what is now Arkansas, Tennessee, Kentucky, and Louisiana. The Indians also burned a certain moss that grew in creeks to produce a salt substitute (Salt Creek in Talladega County, Alabama, probably refers to this practice). They did the same with the stalks of a particular herb, thought to have been an orache (*Atriplex spp.*). Ash of hickory bark also makes an acceptable salt substitute, as any competent woodsman knows.

Sugar could be obtained from the sugar maple simply by tapping the tree and boiling the sap, then letting the syrup evaporate. Most people are familiar with this process, which is still in use today wherever the sugar maple is found. However, few people realize that the same method can be used to produce syrup and sugar from other trees found in the Valley. The best of these are the sycamore, red maple, walnuts, and hickories. The sugar contents of these trees is not quite so high as is found in sugar maple, but the syrup they provide is far better than no sweetener at all.   Honey locust pods were also eaten for their sugar content.

We will examine domestic manufacture and medicines derived from wild plants in a later chapter.

A man was courting a woman and they were seated on the ground at a certain place. Some time afterwards the man came back to the spot and saw a small weed growing up just where the woman had been sitting. He went several times, until the weed got to be of some height.

Now he began to care for it. When it was about a foot high he took off some leaves and smelt of them and they smelt good to him, and others he would throw into the fire, finding the odor they gave forth in burning very agreeable. He cultivated this plant until it gave forth seed.

Tobacco was gotten in this manner, and since this man and woman were very happy when they were there and were very peacefully inclined toward each other, tobacco has ever since been used in concluding peace and friendship among the Indian tribes.

A Creek Tale

VI

Wilderness School
Part Two: Animal Kingdom

As important as plants were in the diet of the Woodland people of the Valley, game animals were the basic source of food. The most important game animal was the white-tailed deer *(Odocoileus virginianus)*, which from very ancient times supplied the bulk of the meat and animal fat consumed by the people. Other animals crucial to the Indians' survival in the Chattahoochee River Valley included the gray squirrel *(Sciurus carolinensis)* and the fox squirrel *(S. niger)*, cottontail rabbit *(Sylvilagus florodamis)*, swamp rabbit *(S. aquaticus)*, and wild turkey *(Meleagris gallapavo)*. Passenger pigeons *(Ectopistes migratorius)* and water fowl were eaten when available, and black bears *(Ursus americanus)* were widely hunted. Bears were hunted as much for their pelts and fat as for their meat--bear oil was the favorite cooking oil among the Indians of the Valley.

Fish were an important source of protein, particularly catfish *(Ictalurus sp.)*, American shad *(Alosa sapidissima)* or Alabama shad *(A. alabamae)*, largemouth bass *(Micropterus salmoides)*, sunfish *(Lepomis sp. and Elassoma sp., plus Enneacanthus gloriosus)*, sturgeon *(Acipenser oxyrhynchus)*, this latter once common in the Chattahoochee but now unknown due to the construction of dams.

Locha-yekcha, *Snapping turtle*

The Indians were also fond of turtles, particularly the snapping turtle *(Chelydra serpentina)*, pond turtle *(Chrysemys Florida)*, box turtle *(Terrapene carolina)* and the gopher tortoise *(Gopherus polyphemus)*, and almost every form of shellfish, from salty Gulf oysters to freshwater mussels. They probably also captured and ate the American alligator

(Alligator mississippiensis) whenever possible.
To this list we should add many small mammals--opossum *(Didelphis virginiana or marsupialis)*, raccoon *(Procyon lotor)*, bobcat *(Felix rufus)*, chipmunk *(Tamias striatus)*, muskrat *(Ondatra zibethicus)*, even striped skunk *(Mephitis mephitis)*. Some authorities report a resistance among historic Indian warriors toward eating opossum for fear that consumption of such a creature would make them slow and dull-witted, but opossum bones are regularly found at early Indian sites in the Valley.
Bobcats and mountain lions or cougars *(Felix concolor)*, the latter called panthers or "painters" by early white settlers in the Valley, were also hunted by the Indians.

Education of Males
Given the importance of game meat to the Indians, it is not surprising that so much emphasis in their culture was placed on training males to hunt. In historic times, young Indian boys were taught to make and handle weapons almost as soon as they could walk. It must have been the same in Woodland and Mississippian times. Boys received specific and detailed training from their elders. Particular emphasis was placed on self-discipline, general woodlore, the manufacture and maintenance of weapons, and mastering animal habits, anatomy, and habitat. Young boys were systematically taught to think like the quarry they sought. Apparently, some individuals specialized in trapping rather than hunting, and others concentrated on the pursuit of particular animals, learning their characteristics and behavior down to the smallest detail. Thus many male Indians were able to ape the behavior of, say, the white-tailed deer or the black bear, even to the point of being able to replicate the creature's vocalizations, body movements, and other mannerisms.
Some knowledge of animal habits and hunting technique was picked up by the boys from listening to the conversations of the men and from tagging along on local hunts whenever allowed.

But the bulk of a boy's wilderness training was more formalized and direct. In hunting societies, males tend to dominate and the clan structure is usually patrilineal--that is, descent is reckoned through the father and other male ancestors. Instruction for the young, particularly the boys, would likely come directly from the father and paternal grandfather and perhaps the father's brothers. In historic times, however, when the Indians of the Valley led a more settled, agricultural life, we know that this training was primarily the responsibility of a boy's maternal uncle, usually his mother's oldest brother. This was because, in the clan structure of the historic period, descent was determined matrilineally. A boy belonged to his mother's clan, not his father's. Discipline and, in a general sense, education, were the province of the dominant clan male on the mother's side--the elder uncle.

Discipline for boys was severe, by our standards, and instruction was stern and constant. It began as soon as the boy could walk and lasted until he became a man--that is, until he earned his adult or war name, usually in his late teens. In the very beginning, when still a child, males were disciplined by their mothers, but this did not last long for fear the boy would become effeminate. As soon as practical, boys left their mothers' care and entered the tutelage of their uncles and other elders. In historic times, young Indian boys were required to immerse themselves in the nearest body of water every morning--winter or summer. Sometimes their lower limbs were scratched with gar's teeth to allow their blood to flow, a process the Indians believed lightened their limbs and made them strong and swift afoot. Seeing their own blood flow also taught the youngsters not to fear injury so much. Most of the time, the skin was moistened thoroughly with water before this type of scratching was done. However, when the boys were being punished for misbehavior, they might be dry scratched--that is, scratched without water.

The point of all this training was to turn boys into mighty hunters, a serious business among people whose survival depended upon the ability of their men to locate and kill game. Of course, such training was ideally suited to producing warriors as well as hunters, and in fact the two appear to have been inseparably intertwined in the minds of the men since time immemorial. In later times, Indian ball play, a particularly rough form of lacrosse, was also used to train and condition boys and young men. We are not certain when ball play began among the early people of the Valley, but there are indications that Woodland Indians had some form of this sport. However, for now we will concern ourselves with woodcraft and hunting. Warfare and ball playing, which the historic Creeks called "the little brother of war," will be treated in later chapters.

Fire Making

One of the first lessons an Indian boy had was in the proper way to construct and start a fire. This seemingly simple task was actually quite complicated--as any outdoorsman or Boy Scout who has mastered even the rudiments of the art can attest. In addition to having to learn how to start a fire through friction, Indian boys had to sort out and master the characteristics of dozens of different kinds of wood and other flammable materials, such as dried and split river cane and birch bark. This task was difficult enough in itself, but among the early people of the Valley, fire was associated with the sun and therefore with spiritual matters, which gave to fire-building a ritual solemnity we sometimes have difficulty appreciating. And, of course, in the winter, wood fires were necessary for survival. Knowing how to start a fire in a driving January rain could mean the difference between life and death or, at the very least, between relative comfort and extreme discomfort. For all these reasons, fire-making was a serious business to the Indians of the Valley. Absolute mastery of the art was required.

Firewood was selected according to several uses, that is, according to whether the fire was to be for warmth, illumination, or cooking, to hollow out a log canoe, to keep mosquitoes or other insects away, to attract fish, to smoke meat, for ceremonial purposes, or for some other use. Wood suitable for one type of fire might not be suitable in another. For example, most pine ignites quickly and produces brief but intense heat. Once fully ignited, pine will continue to burn even in the rain. It requires a considerable downpour to extinguish a fully established pine fire. These characteristics make pine an ideal wood for starting fires and for supplying quick warmth. However, pine is not suitable for cooking because it imparts an unpleasant flavor, tars meats and vessels, and quickly reduces to ash. It also burns so quickly that a large pine fire requires a considerable supply of wood to maintain. On the other hand, hardwoods, such as hickory or oak, are more difficult to ignite than pine, but burn for a long time, producing long-lasting hot coals that impart a savory flavor. They are excellent for cooking and for smoking meat and fish.

Among the many widely available hardwoods in the Valley, hickory and oak make the best cooking fires and night fires. A hickory or oak fire will not smoke excessively if given room to draw underneath, will not tar cooking vessels, and will last long enough to prepare food properly. Hickory and oak coals are easily banked with their own ash and will survive overnight so they can be rekindled in the morning simply by blowing on them. Other high-energy hardwoods found in the Piedmont and Coastal Plain of the Valley include sourwood, serviceberry, hard maple, live oak, beech, plum, persimmon (which the Indians, who were very fond of persimmons, would have been loath to cut), both black and honey locust, holly, witch hazel, the hawthornes, dogwood, birch, and ash. Other Valley hardwoods, such as elm, yellow poplar, cottonwood, sweetgum, sycamore, mulberry, sassafras, and the like, will burn and produce a coal, but they produce far less heat than those listed above. When green, some wood that is highly flammable when dry or seasoned is practically useless for a fire. Green pine, even green pitch pine, burns reluctantly if at all. Valley hardwoods that burn poorly when they are green include basswood, box elder, yellow poplar, sassafras, serviceberry, sycamore, water oak, the gums, persimmon, red maple, red oak, chestnut (no longer available), and butternut. When green, the Indians used these woods for backlogs to reflect heat back onto their sleeping robes. In summer, when the sap is up, few green woods will burn at all.

In addition to mastering the burning characteristics of many different woods, Indian boys had to be aware of other properties. For example, dogwood burns readily and with great warmth, but it pops and can throw hot coals several feet, making it a dangerous wood for indoor fires. The same is true of most pines, chestnut, red cedar, box elder, sassafras, and yellow poplar. Green white pine can be extremely difficult to ignite, but its pine cones burn so readily when seasoned that they can be used as kindling. American holly leaves burst into a bright flame when ignited, making holly branches ideal torches for brief periods. Hickory, which burns readily once downed and split, can be the devil to fell. Many woods are difficult if not impossible to split, especially with primitive stone tools. Among these are sweetgum, honey locust, box elder, the elms, sycamore, and sugar maple. Cottonwood and alder impart a very pleasant taste to fish, as does sassafras. Valley Indians were fond of fish baked with a sprig of cottonwood inserted in its body cavity. And so on.

Therefore, one of the first tasks for the Indian youth was to learn to correctly identify the many different trees found in the Chattahoochee River Valley, a relatively simple matter in the summer when every tree is decked out in its characteristic leaves. In the winter, however, accurate tree identification is a different proposition altogether. It requires the student to master such recondite subjects as bark configuration, tree silhouettes, and wood grains, difficult tasks that can plague even a trained arborist. Yet, being able to tell the difference between deadwood fat pine stripped of its bark and say, driftwood yellow poplar, could mean the difference between getting a fire started in a cold, driving rainstorm--or freezing. At such times, there was little margin for error.

Once the purpose of the fire was known, wood was selected according to its function in the fire. Punk or very fine tinder, used to produce coals in the early stages of friction fire-building, could be made from powdered wood taken from inside standing stumps or from the knots of oaks and hickories or the place where a limb had broken off either of the latter. A fire bundle of extremely light, flammable material was necessary to catch the coals so they could be blown into a flame. Each fire-builder probably had his own favorite materials for a fire bundle. Dried strips of cedar bark, especially when mixed with cattail down, make an excellent fire bundle. River birch bark and cattail down will also work. In fact, river birch bark stripped directly from the tree is good tinder. Dried and pulverized, it makes suitable punk. Dead or very dry Spanish moss will also burn readily and may have been used as a fire bundle in dry weather. Most kindling, which was ignited by flames from the fire bundle and, in turn, set fire to the larger firewood, was struck from pine knots--actually, from where limbs joined pine trees--the same "lighterd" or fat pine we use today. As long as the tree is dead, it makes no difference whether it is standing or on the ground.

Most fires were started by friction, either by rubbing two dried sticks together very vigorously for 10 to 15 minutes or by using a flat base board and a sharpened drill. In the latter method, which was quite common, a shallow hole was cut into a dry piece of hardwood--say yellow poplar or cottonwood--and the point of a sharpened stick or drill was inserted into the hole. The historic Creeks seem to have preferred slippery elm for a fire stick. It is crucial that both fire board and fire stick be dry and free of vegetable or animal oils, including that imparted from contact with human skin. By applying pressure to the stick and twirling it rapidly and continuously between the palms, intense heat was produced where the point rubbed against the sides of the hole. A little fire punk was placed in the hole, and as the friction produced greater heat, the punk ignited. The glowing coals were then transferred to the fire bundle--say, cedar strips and cattail down--and blown upon until it burst into flames. Very small splinters of fat pine or lighterd were quickly added until the fire was hot enough to burn small twigs of hardwood mixed with pine. Very gradually, as the flames increased in intensity and the hardwoods cast a few coals, the size of the wood applied to the fire was increased. The secret to Indian fire-building was in knowing the characteristics of the different woods and having the patience to begin with very small bits of kindling and gradually add more and larger sticks to the flame. Most people want to add large logs to a beginning fire immediately, and they laboriously chop and saw stacks of wood for that purpose. Thus an inexperienced woodsman will have piles of fire logs in camp, a little kindling, and almost no finger wood. Indians spent their time gathering kindling and large stacks of finger wood--sometimes called squaw wood--which they added to the fire in strict gradation. Whenever possible, they avoided ground wood and selected their squaw wood from the lower branches of standing dead trees.

With a hot bed of hardwood coals, almost any wood, no matter how green, could be burned. To avoid having to get up repeatedly during the night, Valley Indians cut long night logs-- which they placed across the coals and which they could nudge into the fire from their sleeping robes. If they wanted instant illumination, they could throw a handful of holly leaves into the flames. To drive away mosquitoes, wax myrtle leaves were thrown on the fire.

In historic times, Indians allowed their fires to die out or banked them with ash or sand. It was considered a serious offense against nature to pour water on a fire. Fire and water were two entirely separate and distinct primary elements and were never to be mixed. This is a reminder that, to Valley Indians, fire was directly associated with the sun and, as such, had a spiritual significance it does not have for us.

Staying Found

After learning how to identify useful plants and trees and to build a fire correctly, an Indian boy had to master many other basics of woodcraft essential to the hunt.   One of the most important of these was learning to move through the wilderness, often for several hundred miles, without getting lost.   This seems a mysterious process, and much nonsense has been written about it, until we realize that to the Indians the process was not so much a matter of not getting lost as staying found.   In short, the wilderness through which they moved was not a wilderness to them.   They were guided by rivers and tributary water courses, game trails, geographical features--ridges, mountains, valleys, large rocks, distinctive trees--to which we now pay scant attention.   Indians also looked up, which we seldom do anymore unless it is through a telescope.   They knew the position of the fixed stars, could identify and had names for many of the constellations, and were constantly aware of their orientation in regard to the four cardinal directions.   This latter is another example of the power of spiritual matters in their life: the sun (and to a lesser degree, the moon) was an object of veneration for the early people of the Valley from at least the Woodland Period on.   Its whereabouts at all times was of paramount importance.   In addition to the four cardinal directions, Valley Indians divided the compass into at least four more points, namely northwest, northeast, southwest, and southeast.   One way they did this was through observation of such naturally occurring repetitive elements as prevailing winds--from the southwest in our area--cold winds, rain-laden winds, and the like.   Moreover, their extensive knowledge of plant and animal life provided them with a portable backdrop to all their movements.   Whether they could always find a certain type of moss that grows only on the north side of trees is debatable, but they would certainly have recognized minute changes in flora and fauna as general guides for direction.

Within the Chattahoochee River Valley itself, the river and it tributaries were roadways over which the Indians could move with ease and confidence.   Followed downstream, almost every trickle of water led to a creek and every creek to the river itself. Frequently, as is the case with Upatoi Creek and Uchee Creek, these tributaries could be followed to their headwaters, from which it was but a short trek to the headwaters of other streams leading to entirely different river systems--in this case, the Flint and Tallapoosa Rivers, respectively. By this method, it was possible for the Woodland people to travel hundreds of miles away from their villages on the Chattahoochee without getting lost. As the centuries passed, trade routes and pathways to favorite hunting grounds became well established and a considerable body of geographical knowledge was accumulated.

As a final point, it should be recognized that, to an Indian, getting lost in the woods was an entirely different experience than it is for us today. Unless he were injured or sick, a lost Indian hunter was in no particular danger. The forest around him was thick with wild plants that would help sustain life and even provide raw materials to help him repair his clothes and moccasins. He had his weapons, with which he could down game. He could start a fire with two sticks and a handful of pine splinters. He had been building impromptu shelters of sticks and leaves and sleeping in them all his life. Spending a few nights or even weeks in such a home would have held no terrors for him. Water was usually readily obtainable in the Southeast. Even in times of drought, an Indian knew he could obtain clean, pure drinking water by tapping certain trees--maples, hickories, or sycamores. In short, there was no reason for the Indian hunter to feel the panic that grips many contemporary outdoorsmen--and often leads to their death--when they get turned around in the woods.

Bow and Arrow

With these elemental woodland skills in hand, the Indian boy was ready to attempt to master the hunt, a demanding pursuit that often required him to be abroad in all kinds of inclement weather, often far from home, with the survival of his family and his village at stake. The proper weapons to do the job were essential, and every Indian boy spent many hours learning to make and repair his own weapons.

The bow and arrow, which replaced the spear and atlatl toward the end of the Woodland Period, must have greatly increased the Indians' efficiency at downing deer and small game, including birds and water fowl. The bow and arrow had been discovered around 10,000 B.C. in Europe, but it did not appear in America and the Chattahoochee River Valley until some time after A.D. 700. No one can say for sure how it was discovered, but it would not have been possible without the Woodland peoples' intimate knowledge of the characteristics of various types of wood. Centuries of experience with wooden-handled or wood-shafted weapons of all sorts lay behind the development of the bow and arrow.

Making a bow was one of the most difficult wilderness skills to learn. Even today, using modern, steel-bladed tools, it is a tedious and frustrating task, and many attempts end in failure. Not just any wood would do. West of the Mississippi, the preferred wood for bows was osage orange. But in the East, in the Chattahoochee River Valley and adjacent areas, the favorite wood for bows was the black locust, cut green, allowed to cure, and then carefully shaped. Flint knives, wood wrenches fashioned from animal bone, or perhaps the tooth of a beaver fastened to a hickory handle, were used to shape the bow. If black locust could not be obtained, sassafras was often used, as were witch hazel, cedar, mulberry, or hickory. Bows were stout and roughly triangular in cross-section. They were the same height as the individual who used them. Proud owners rubbed them with bear's oil until they gleamed. Many were decorated with bright colors or inlaid with pearls.

Arrows were made from river cane *(Arundinaria gigantea)*, an immensely important plant to Valley Indians, or dogwood *(Cornus spp.)*. They were carefully fashioned to be of equal diameter from one end to the other. The notched end of the shaft was fletched with hawk, eagle, or wild turkey feathers. Sometimes their tips were merely sharpened and then hardened in fire, but most often they were tipped with bits of flint, deer

antler, bone, garfish
teeth, or any hard
material that would
take a point. Hunters
and warriors carried
raw materials and
tool kits with which
to make arrowheads
on the spot. Bow
strings were made of

twisted deer hide, occasionally of bear gut or squirrel hide.
They were of excellent quality and performed as well as modern
bow strings of synthetic fibers--unless, of course, it rained.

For quivers, the early Indians used a variety of animal hides
or simply went afield with arrows clutched in their bow hand or
stuck in their hair.

The bow and arrow was an extremely efficient and powerful
weapon in the hands of skilled archers. As a consequence, it
quickly replaced the hand spear and atlatl as the weapon of
choice among Valley Indians.

Another weapon probably in wide use in the Valley by
Woodland times was the blowgun, the idea for which was
perhaps originally imported from Mexico or South America. It,
too, was made from river cane, necessarily very straight, that
had been hollowed out to a length of from six to 10 feet. Darts
were made from slender pieces of hard yellow pine or from thin
cane. The darts, which were slightly over a foot in length, were
fletched with thistledown and their tips were sharpened and
hardened in fire. Of limited range, blowguns were the favorite
hunting weapons of boys in pursuit of squirrels, rabbits, and
birds.

So equipped, the young Woodland hunter began his quest of
meat for the pot. Starting with small game--squirrel, rabbits,
and birds--which he downed with his blowgun or bow and
arrow, he progressed to raccoon, and opossum, muskrat, and
perhaps even beaver. At each step of the way, he became

Blow guns were effective at short range.

progressively schooled in animal behavior and increasingly skilled with his weapons.

During this stage, the youngster would also be learning to trap, to prepare deadfalls, and to spring traps rigged from vegetable fiber and a bent-over sapling. Unfortunately, not a great deal of information has come down to us on trapping because the materials used were perishable. However, in Indian myths we hear of monstrous creatures, perhaps mountain lions, being trapped in deep pits covered with vegetation. Bears, fearsome adversaries when cornered, may also have been trapped in this manner.

When he was finally strong enough, the young Indian male might be allowed to accompany his mother to recover meat killed by his father or uncle or perhaps to go along in some menial capacity on part of an actual hunt. One of the proudest days of his life would be when he was asked by the men to accompany them on a hunt as an equal. For a strong and able boy this might come as soon as his 12th or 13th birthday.

Great Winter Hunt

Although the early Indians of the Valley hunted any time they needed meat, certain seasons of the year were better for hunting than others. For example, during the fall rut, deer tended to follow a behavioral pattern that made them easy to locate and kill. Turkeys were fatter after consuming the acorns and nuts of the fall mast. Bears tend to den in the colder winter months. And so on. After European contact and the establishment of the deer skin and fur trade, seasonal hunting became more fixed. Deer hunting, which had heretofore been a year-around activity tied to survival, became a commercial enterprise, a development which radically altered the lifestyle of Valley Indians and eventually led to the near extinction of the animal upon which that lifestyle was based. However, what little we know of the hunting techniques of Valley Indians comes from the period after European contact. The amount of game taken was certainly different after the establishment of the hide and fur trade, but the basic hunting methods would not have differed much from those practiced in Woodland times.

For Valley Indians in historic times the winter hunt usually began in October, although preparations for it were started much sooner, and ended in March. The women were busy for weeks in advance, preparing food and clothing for the men to take along. Each man was provisioned with an adequate supply of dried meat, persimmon bread, and, toward the end of the Woodland Period, parched corn. The men reworked their weapons, tested and polished their bows, and selected only their best and truest arrows for the hunt. Sometimes women accompanied their husbands so they could bring the meat back to camp and begin the process of cleaning and curing the skins immediately. No matter who went, they were expected to be able to cover 25 to 30 miles a day at a steady trot and to be able to endure all the discomforts of winter while on the move.

The primary quarry was the white-tailed deer, which the Indians killed for meat and skins. They stalked deer singly or in groups. Many hunters carried a dried and cleaned deer head with the skin and antlers attached. The antlers were carefully hollowed out to make them light, and the skin was so fashioned that it would conceal a considerable portion of the hunter's body. So outfitted, he could sneak up close to his quarry, using all his

Eacho, *White-tailed deer*

skill at imitating the creature's movements and sounds, before rising suddenly to snap off a killing shot.

Deer were also taken by setting fire to a section of the forest and either driving the animals toward a point of land or gradually forcing them into a surround of hunters. In either case, the terrified creatures were usually easy prey. When possible, drivers pushed the deer onto promontories in lakes or rivers and then into the water where hunters in canoes dispatched them quickly. In all likelihood, however, the Indians of the Valley would have been circumspect about starting fires, particularly in an area of mature hardwoods. They would have been well aware that hickories and oaks can require more than 20 years to begin bearing nuts and acorns-- longer than that to reach peak production stage.

Authorities differ on the whether buffalo *(Bison bison)* were present in the Valley in the past. There are reports of buffalo being sighted near the Valley in historic times, but no remains of buffalo kills or any bones have been found in the Valley. Certainly there were large herds in the area now occupied by Kentucky, Arkansas, and Tennessee. Valley Indians would not have hesitated to seek them even in such distant places. Buffalo meat was a great favorite of Native Americans and buffalo robes were preferred bedding wherever they could be obtained. Buffalo hide was also made into shields, breastplates, and headdresses. Perhaps Valley Indians traded to obtain buffalo skins.

Bear could be found closer to home. In the winter, their customary den was in the hollows of trees. The Indians located them by searching for telltale signs of claw marks on the tree trunks. Once located, it was fairly easy to smoke the bears out of their dens and shoot them as they emerged. They might also be trapped at such times. After the delicious fat was rendered into oil, it was stored in gourds or deerskin containers. The Indians used it for frying and flavoring, anointed their bodies and hair with it, and rubbed it on their bows. The hides made good bedding and warm winter coats. The meat was eaten well done--Southeastern Indians ate all their meat cooked thoroughly. There is no evidence that the Indians made bacon out of bear until they were taught to do so by Europeans. It is also not true that the Indians of the Valley hunted for bear in honey trees, at least during prehistoric times. There were no honey bees in the Valley until bee cultivation began in the historic period.

Turkeys were hunted when they were fat from the fall mast. Turkey calls were made out of the hollow secondary wing bone of the creature, or the Indians simply cupped their palms and imitated the gobbler. Turkeys could be taken quite close to home because the Chattahoochee River Valley was, and still is, prime gobbler country.

It is likely that other animals, such as the beaver, otter, raccoon and rabbit, were trapped as well as shot. Pachee, the *passenger pigeon is extinct.* Passenger pigeons were killed as much for their oil as meat. When the Indians located a pigeon roost, where thousands of the fat birds roosted in a single tree, they would wait until nightfall. Then, using torches to light their work, they would approach the roost and knock the birds out of the tree with long poles. Hundreds of pigeons might be taken in this manner in one night.

Passenger pigeons were also taken with nets and traps.

Fishing

Southeastern Indians appear to have been fond of both fish and shellfish, and the early people of the Valley were no exception. In addition to freshwater mussels and clams, Valley Indians ate catfish, bream, bass, drum, sturgeon, and shad with great relish, often throwing fish fries and dances when a particularly good catch was made.

Every spring during historic times, the people of Cusseta and Coweta would come to fish at the falls where Columbus and Phenix City are now located. The falls and riffles on the west side of the river belonged to the people of Coweta; those on the east, to Cusseta. We have no idea how old the custom was when it was first observed by Europeans, but it must have gone back to at least the Woodland Period. Sometimes the Indians used dip or scoop nets attached to the ends of long poles, positioning themselves on rocks above the runs on either side of the river. Often they shot the fish with long arrows or speared them with sharpened cane shafts whose tips had been hardened in fire. Some men possessed spears tipped with the barb of a sting ray or the tail of a horseshoe crab.

Other methods used by the Woodland Indians to catch fish included gill nets, fish weirs made of fiber and bark strips, rock traps, and poison. Sometimes they built fires in their canoes to attract fish at night and speared or shot them with arrows when they rose to the surface. They set out trot lines just as we do, using a piece of meat or a doughball for bait. A small, sharpened piece of bone or wood, shaped like a toothpick, often served as a hook. The line was attached to the middle of the hook, which was then covered by the bait. When the fish swallowed the bait and jerked on the line, the hook would turn crosswise in the fish's stomach and hold securely.

A favorite method of fishing was to construct V-shaped rock traps in the river with the pointed end downstream and open. Inside the opening was a smaller V, with the pointed end, also open, facing upstream. Fish could easily find their way into such a trap, but they were usually unable to get back out. During times of low water, it was a simple matter to drive them into the shallows where they could be speared or shot with arrows. Fish baskets made of oak or hickory bark and cane and constructed on the same principle as the rock traps were also widely used.

Sturgeon were taken when they were discovered floating on the surface. The Indians would loop a piece of line about the great fish's tail and hang on. Aroused, a large sturgeon was capable of pulling a strong man under the water, and tremendous battles were waged until the fish tired. Sturgeon provided both flesh and roe, as did shad. Great hauls of shad were once taken from the river, but the construction of massive dams in our era has greatly reduced their numbers. The same dams have eliminated sturgeon altogether.

As summer progressed and the waters of the river and its creeks receded, larger fish collected in the remaining pools of deep water. At such times, they might be taken by a group of men dragging nets through the pools, but most often they were poisoned. To accomplish the latter, the Valley Indians used either the buckeye (*Aesculus spp.*) or the devil's shoestring (*Tephrosia spp.*). Both possess a rotenone-like poison that is readily extracted by crushing or pounding the plant. The Indians drove wooden piles in the river pools or creek beds and, using wooden mallets, pounded the plants and nuts on top of the stakes until the residue began to drip into the water. In a matter of minutes, stunned fish would began to rise to the surface where they were easily scooped up and tossed ashore. Hundreds of fish might be taken in a single afternoon in this manner. Some would be saved for drying or smoking and the rest baked, broiled, or fried on the spot.

A favorite method of preparing bass and shad was to gut them, place a cottonwood twig in the body cavity for flavoring, then coat them with mud and bake them in hot coals.

By all such methods did the Woodland people feed themselves

for thousands of years, from long before the birth of Christ to the beginnings of the Mississippian Period. It is easy to forget that, in our fascination with their burial customs and religious ceremonies, the Woodland people--and those who followed them in the Valley--had to eat, clothe themselves, and take care of their everyday needs. For the average person, survival was still a struggle. It is well to keep this in mind when reading the following chapters on the Mississippian era, the last great flowering of American Indian civilization in our area before the coming of the white man.

Late Prehistoric
700 - 1600

The birds challenged the four-footed animals to a great ball play. It was agreed that all creatures which had teeth should be on one side and all those which had feathers should go on the other side with the birds.

The day was fixed and all the arrangements were made; the ground was prepared, the poles erected, and the balls conjured by the medicine men.

When the animals came, all that had teeth went on one side and the birds on the other. At last the bat came. He went with the animals having teeth, but they said:

"No, you have wings, you must go with the birds." He went to the birds and they said: "No, you have teeth, you must go with the animals." So they drove him away, saying: "You are so little you could do no good."

He went to the animals and begged that they would permit him to play with them. They finally said, "You are too small to help us, but as you have teeth we will let you remain on our side."

The play began and it soon appeared that the birds were winning, as they could catch the ball in the air, where the four-footed animals could not reach it. The Crane was the best player. The animals were in despair, as none of them could fly. The little Bat now flew into the air and caught the ball as the Crane was flapping slowly along. Again and again the bat caught the ball, and he won the game for the four-footed animals.

They agreed that though he was so small he should always be classed with the animals having teeth.

A Creek Tale

VII

Mississippian Period
700-1600

Mississippian platform mound

The Mississippian Period, so named because of the tremendous mound complexes from this period found in the Mississippi River Valley, was a time of intense social and religious activity, full of pomp and ceremony, and, if anything, of even more elaborate ritual than the preceding Woodland Period. The Spanish explorers of the 16th century encountered evidence of this once-great Indian civilization throughout North Florida, Georgia, Alabama, Tennessee, and the Carolinas. In fact, some of the ceremonial mound centers functioned until the early 17th century, although the vast majority appear to have gone into sharp decline much sooner. Initially, archaeologists attributed this decline to conquest by an invading group of Native Americans, supposedly, in our area, the historic Muskogulgi or Creeks. However, new evidence suggests that epidemics of European and African diseases, introduced by contact diffusion from the Caribbean following Columbus's initial voyage in 1492, may have decimated the Mississippian people in the Southeast, including those who once inhabited the Chattahoochee River Valley.

Fortunately, the archaeological record from the period is extensive in the Chattahoochee River Valley. From these remains, and from accounts of early Spanish and French explorers, who first came into contact with the Mississippian people in the 16th century, we can reconstruct a much more detailed picture of daily life in the Valley than has been possible for any previous period.

Once again, the ultimate impetus for this culture seems to have come from the west, perhaps from Mexico or Central America. There are distinct similarities between the platform mounds built by the Mississippian people and the pre-Columbian pyramids found in Mexico. And the Mississippian people in the Chattahoochee River Valley were almost certainly influenced by people living at the great platform mound centers in what is now the central United States, including those near Cahokia, Illinois, and Spiro, Oklahoma, and, more immediately, at Etowah in North Georgia, the Macon Plateau in Central Georgia, and Moundville, Alabama.

Some authorities think the Mississippian sites on the Chattahoochee were established by people radiating outward from what is now Alabama, perhaps as emigrants from a powerful chiefdom. This movement might explain the moats and palisades protecting many Mississippian sites in the Valley, necessary defenses against a displaced indigenous population. Other authorities believe Mississippian culture, including its religious beliefs and paradigms for social organization, was primarily spread through a process of contact diffusion. One way this could have happened is through the widespread trade network that may have linked the civilizations of Mesoamerica with the Mississippi River Valley mound centers, including those in Ohio and Illinois, and that most certainly linked the latter with mound centers on the Chattahoochee and elsewhere in the

Southeast.   It has even been suggested that a group of traders,
known to the Aztecs as *pochteca*, may have been frequent
visitors among the native people of the American Midwest.
Some of these traders may have settled there, bringing with them
foreign notions of social ranking, religion, and even human
sacrifice.   In turn, these new ideas reached the Chattahoochee
via the old trade routes that had connected the Valley people
with the Midwest populations since at least early Woodland
times.

Mississippian Settlements

However they were settled, Mississippian villages were
usually situated on large rivers or streams.   They appear to have
been placed so as to make them adjacent to rich bottomlands,
for farming, and accessible to diverse ecosystems--uplands,
coastal plain, Gulf coast--which allowed for maximum
exploitation of natural resources.   The sites are marked by huge,
rectangular, flat-topped platform or temple mounds which served
as bases for religious reliquaries, charnel houses, elite
residences, or council houses.   Often these platform mounds
were arrayed around open plazas.   Extensive village areas
surrounded the plazas.   Sometimes the entire site was surrounded
by a moat and palisade, an indication either that the settlements
were made in hostile territory or that they were threatened by
other groups in the area.

There is clear indication in the composition of the mounds
and in the archaeological materials recovered from them that the
Mississippian Period was marked by a high degree of religious
and secular ceremonialism.   For example, buildings or structures
on the summits of the mounds were periodically deliberately
dismantled or burned, then covered with earth upon which new
structures were built.   The mounds themselves frequently show
evidence of rebuilding, with successive caps of clay and sand
being heaped over the summits at irregular intervals.   Authorities
speculate that religious beliefs during the Mississippian Period
were centered around agriculture and the importance of corn as

a food crop. There is evidence of the worship of a fire-sun diety, just as in the preceding Woodland period. Perhaps the sun was represented on earth by an elite priest or chief. There is no doubt that certain individuals or "Big Men" enjoyed elite status and were buried with elaborate ritual in recognition of their position. In some fashion as yet not completely understood, recapping of the mounds and burial of human skeletons or bone bundles appear to have been related. It is known that Mississippian people preserved the skeletal remains of their leaders, sometimes collecting these into bone bundles and storing them in mortuary buildings or charnel houses on the summits of the mounds. At least one student of the subject, Vernon J. Knight, Jr., believes the periodic rebuilding and recapping of the mounds had to do with cremation and burial of human remains for the purpose of propitiating the spirits of the dead and banishing the evil karma that had supposedly accumulated on the site.

However, platform mound building is only one of the traits that distinguishes Mississippian culture. The appearance of extensive river bottom agriculture is another feature which sets the Mississippian people off from their predecessors. The platform mound builders were not only hunters and gatherers of wild food, but they were also farmers who cultivated seed plants, corn, pumpkins, beans, squash, and probably tobacco in large fields along the banks of the Chattahoochee.

By observing where wild plants grew best, and by trial and error, the Indians of the Valley discovered that bottomland soils produced better and bigger crops. Periodic flooding assured regular restoration of nutrients in the soil along the river and its tributaries.

Corn Culture

Mississippian people continued to grow and experiment with wild seed plants, just as they had done during the Woodland Period. However, corn--actually a form of maize--was the most important crop grown by the Valley Indians in Mississippian times. They became increasingly dependent upon a good crop for survival, so much so that the cultivation, planting, and harvesting of the annual corn crop assumed a primary role in the people's social, economic, and religious life. The planting and harvesting of the corn crop were times of communal effort and celebration, occasions for socializing, ball play, and other games. Important civic and religious ceremonies were associated with the harvest. Corn was king in the Valley long before cotton.

Ordinary people might have garden patches of their own around their homes, but they were required to take part in cultivating, planting, tending, and harvesting the communal corn fields. In fact, the whole village--men, women and children-- was involved. However, the planting of the annual village corn crop was too crucial to be left to private individuals. Each village seems to have had one person, perhaps a priest or shaman closely associated with the sun god or the plant kingdom, who was in charge of the annual corn crop. At the time he thought proper, he would summon the people by blowing on a conch shell or beating on a drum. Then he would lead them in procession to the fields to be planted.

The Mississippian people possessed no draft animals or beasts of burden--the modern horse was not introduced into the Southeast until the Spanish came in the 16th century. Clearing of the land was done by hand. When necessary, the men used stone axes to fell trees, a laborious process at best. Underbrush was burned off. So far as is known, there was no plowing. Cultivation was done with a hoe often consisting of a wooden pole with the shoulder blade of some large animal affixed to the business end. The men cultivated the soil and the women planted. Planting took place in the spring, probably in late April or early May after the last frost. Women used long pointed sticks to make shallow holes in the ground. Seeds were dropped into the holes and covered with a few inches of soil. Women, old men, and especially boys watched over these communal fields. As the corn began to grow, women picked weeds and boys stood guard duty to scare away the crows and other pests. At night, men patrolled the fields to keep out deer and bears, the latter being particularly fond of the succulent young corn.

In historic times corn was an indispensable food crop for Valley Indians, so much so that the annual harvest was the time of their most important religious festival, the *Poskeeta* or Green Corn Ceremony. It is likely that the *Poskeeta*, which is a ceremony of ritual cleansing, purification, and renewal, was first observed in the Mississippian Period in mid-July at the time the first corn was harvested.

Corn became Valley's most important crop.

Sofkee

Although Valley Indians ate corn prepared much the way we do--boiled or roasted on the ear, ground into cornmeal and baked or fried into bread or fritters--their basic corn dish was a thin hominy gruel called *sofkee*. It was made from thoroughly dried corn kernels which were first soaked in water containing lye. The lye was made by pouring water over hardwood ashes in a container with a small hole in the bottom. After the lye-drip had softened the kernels and loosened the hulls, the corn was placed in a mortar, usually made from a section of a hardwood tree, and then pounded with a hickory pestle until the hulls separated from the sweetmeats. The hulls were completely removed from the kernels in a flat fanner basket, and then the soft corn was either boiled whole or reduced to a paste and then boiled. The resulting mixture was white *sofkee*, *sofkee-hatkee* to the Creeks. Sometimes they allowed the mixture to ferment slightly, producing *sofkee-toksee*, "sour sofkee."

No matter what its final form, a gourd filled with *sofkee* was kept hanging near the door of the dwelling, and the Indians simply helped themselves when they wished by using a wooden dipper attached to the gourd. *Sofkee* was usually taken cold although the women sometimes added it to hot soups and stews.

Community Life

During the Mississippian Period, community life reached a high point of development. Daily life was perhaps more advanced and more comfortable than at any time before or since for the native people of the Valley. The great platform mounds were surrounded by extensive villages of neat huts constructed of sapling uprights lathed with river cane daubed with clay--the so-called wattle and daub technique--that were great improvements over earlier domiciles made of sticks and animal skins. Farming and maximum exploitation of wild food sources, including storage of surplus corn, nuts, berries and fruits, assured a steady food supply, thus freeing males from some of the tyranny of the hunt and women from constant foraging for wild foods. It would be a mistake, however, to think that life was suddenly easy for the people of the Chattahoochee River Valley, especially by today's standards, or that all the people shared equally in the benefits of the society. Women, in particular, worked very hard.

The Work of Women

In addition to child-bearing and -rearing, Indian women were responsible for much of the new agricultural labor, for tending their own family's garden plot, and for almost all domestic chores and home industry. This latter included cleaning and preparing food, making pots and other cooking utensils, cleaning and curing hides and converting them into clothing, and continuing to collect wild plant foods. Domestic manufacture occupied much of their time. From the inner bark of the mulberry tree and from basswood bark and the bark of the slippery elm women made thread and rope, wove a kind of cloth, and made netting for their own hair. Sometimes they turned Spanish moss into thread and the thread into garments. They made baskets, trays, sifters, sieves, and mats from split river cane and oak or hickory splints, often staining the splints with a black walnut dye.

If contemporary examples of Creek basketry are any indication, and they probably are, the baskets made by the Indian women of the Valley were simply  plaited and usually without handles or top. The manufacturing process was a laborious one. First, the women went into the extensive canebrakes that grew along the river and near the mouths of many creeks, selected cane about the size of their fingers, and split it lengthwise into several pieces. The bark was stripped from the cane and then bundled and taken back to the village. There it was soaked in warm water to make it more pliable. Usually a simple over and under weave was used, but at some point in the past the women began to add a characteristic double-false braided rim. The finished products were among the most important and functional domestic utensils the woman owned. She would use her large baskets to store corn, her fanner to separate cracked corn from its husk, and her sifter to make corn meal, all regular daily tasks for native women in the Valley.

Making and firing pots was another constant task, for the clay vessels shattered with distressing frequency, as the many thousands of potsherds found throughout the Valley today attest. Making cooking pots and other domestic vessels was a more difficult job than might at first appear. Not only did the women have to locate and dig their clay, but they also had to mould and dry the pots and then stand watch as they were fired. Hickory bark seems to have been the preferred fuel for firing because it produced high heat that lasted for a long time. Women also gathered the wood for cooking fires, a job which often required them to journey far from home.

How Buckskin Was Made

One of their toughest jobs was the cleaning and preparation of animal hides. Prior to the coming of the white man, almost all hides were converted into clothing or sleeping robes. Some were made into rawhide or fashioned into pouches, bowstrings, and the like. Almost any animal hide could be used in some fashion, but the most sought after were those of the deer, bear, and perhaps buffalo. Of these three, the skin of the white-tailed deer was by far the most important. Women fashioned almost every article of everyday clothing from deer hide, working it and working it until it was as smooth and supple as cloth. The process by which they converted raw deer hide into buckskin differed slightly from individual to individual, but it was always laborious and included the following steps:

As soon as possible, the skin was removed from the dead animal. Women often accompanied their men on deer hunts and hauled the carcass back to camp where they skinned the animal. Sometimes the men would bring in the skins. Either way, timing was of the essence, especially if the weather was warm or damp. As soon as the skin was removed, it was placed in a creek or river to soak for four or five days. The soaking would loosen the hair and soften the black epidermis on the hide. If several skins were being treated simultaneously, they would be weighted down with rocks.

Following a thorough soaking, the hides were placed across a log or a bent sapling to grain--that is, to remove the hair and the dark epidermis. Almost any instrument with a square edge would do for this part of the processing, provided it was not so sharp it could accidentally cut through the hide. To grain their deer hides, Indian women used clam shells, fire-tempered hardwood knives or endscrapers made of flint or split river cane. The idea was to scrape the hair and dark skin away by pulling them down with the hair grain.

After graining, which could take quite a bit of elbow grease, a sharp flint knife was used to flesh the skin completely.   Skilled women could remove every speck of flesh from the hide and were adept at working the skin down to a uniform thickness. Then the skin was dried in the shade and soaked again overnight.   The next morning it was taken out and

Scraping hair off deer hide.

worked by hand, being twisted, stretched, jerked, and sometimes even chewed on by the women until soft as cloth.

At this point, fresh deer brains were rubbed into the skin to further soften it and help cure the hide.   Some Indian women mixed the brains with water so the mixture would spread and penetrate better, and almost all Indian women kept little cakes of dried deer brains handy for this stage of the processing in case fresh brains were not available. In historic times, corn juice was sometimes substituted for brains, but this is a relatively modern development. The now-softened hide might be soaked repeatedly in the brain solution, being wrung out, stretched, and kneaded after each soaking.   The women repeated this stage of the process over and over until they were satisfied that the skin, which would now be quite white and as soft as chamois cloth, was ready to be smoked.

Smoking gave the skin the desired dusky color, helped make it rain-resistant, and increased the likelihood of it drying out soft and supple after being wet.   No heat was allowed to reach the hide, just smoke from a small smudge fire of hardwood punk or perhaps corn cobs. After this, the skins were set aside to season before being turned into skirts, blouses, shirts, leggings, moccasins, quivers, and many other useful articles.

Thus, Valley Indians did not tan their hides with tannic water or other chemicals as we do. They simply worked and worked them until the fibers were broken down and the skin thoroughly "cured." It was hard work, and when the winter hunt was successful, Indian women were kept busy for many weeks processing deer skins.

Men seem to have benefited more than women from the changes taking place in Mississippian society. Although most Valley Indians of which we have any knowledge reckoned their descent through the distaff side, Indian society was distinctly paternalistic. Indian men continued to be trained as hunters and warriors, and those not occupied with administrative or spiritual duties spent much of their time on the hunt or the warpath. Indeed, it was partly through their mastery of the hunt that a more settled existence of the people was made possible. Despite having to perform most of the daily labor, even women must have had more time to themselves. With more leisure time, the arts flourished. No one who has seen the remarkable carvings and beautifully finished implements produced by the Indians of the period can doubt the high degree of skill of these "primitive" craftsmen, who were masters of wood, stone, bone, shell, and clay.

Southeastern Ceremonial Complex

Some of the most beautiful and interesting artwork from the Mississippian Period is found in the symbols and artifacts associated with the Southeastern Ceremonial Complex. This complex of painted or carved symbols, ceremonial objects, god-animal representations, and costume paraphernalia, which appears at mound centers from the Great Lakes to Florida and is especially well-represented at Spiro, Etowah, and Moundville, was originally called the Southern Cult. Archaeologists and anthropologists initially thought the symbols and other elements of the complex indicated the existence of a shared system of religious beliefs among Mississippian people throughout the Southeast. Now, however, students of the subject are more inclined to view the complex in a secular light. Some Southeastern Ceremonial Complex motifs may represent spontaneous expressions of the people's mythology and folk beliefs. Others appear to relate to fertility, war, and political authority. Still others may represent plants or be symbols of animal gods, often anthropomorphized, feared, and venerated by Indians throughout the region.

Whatever its particular function, the Southeastern Ceremonial Complex is a fascinating element of the daily life of the Mississippian people, including those who lived in the Chattahoochee River Valley. Symbols of the complex, which appear painted or incised on ceramic vessels and discs, carved into marine shells, and embossed on copper ornaments and plates, include the cross, the sun circle, the bi-lobed arrow, the ogee, the forked eye, the open eye, the barred oval, the hand and eye, and various death motifs. God-animal figures, such as the eagle, rattlesnake, cat, spider, and other anthropomorphized creatures, also appear with frequency at Mississippian mound sites. Ceremonial objects associated with the complex include shell and copper gorgets, mask gorgets, embossed copper plates, copper hair emblems, ear spools, celts, the monolithic axe, batons or "pole spuds," effigy pipes and effigy bowls and bottles, and engraved conch shell bowls or drinking cups. Costuming, as represented carved into shell or copper or as individual figures, is fantastical, and includes antlered headdresses, the bi-lobed arrow hair emblem, various beaded ornaments, sashes, and the so-called fringed apron. Among the paraphernalia associated with such costumed figures are the baton, flint knife, human head, and hafted celt. These symbols, which are most often found within mounds, and are usually, but not exclusively, associated with burials, are highly stylized. They occur with far too much frequency to be coincidental either in design or in distribution.

The particular meaning of the iconography may not yet be understood, but the Southeastern Ceremonial Complex is composed of a clearly recognizable set of symbols, a circumstance that points toward the existence, in Mississippian times, of a widespread, underlying way of looking at the world, a *weltanschaung*, to use the German word. Such a comprehensive view of the world as is indicated by the Southeastern Ceremonial Complex hints at a rich mythological life among Mississippian people, itself indicative of a shared and deeply felt sense of cultural identity. In other words, what we may properly call a civilization existed among native American people of the Southeast, including those in the Chattahoochee River Valley, just prior to the arrival of Europeans in the New World.

Emergence of Riverine Chiefdoms
In ways we don't fully understand, the Southeastern Ceremonial Complex may relate to another major development of the Mississippian Period: the centralization of political authority and the emergence of powerful leaders, the so-called Big Men of anthropological literature.

Large Mississippian mound centers, such as those at Moundville, Etowah, and Macon, were administrative and religious centers organized into hierarchical riverine chiefdoms with sovereignty over extensive territory, including prime hunting and agricultural lands, large populations, far-flung colonies, and secondary mound centers. These were highly structured societies, with powerful chiefs--Big Men--and high status kinship groups that dominated the life of the common people through both civic and religious power. The chroniclers of the expedition of Hernando DeSoto through the Southeast (1539-42) recorded the names of several of these chiefdoms, among them Apalachee in northern Florida, Oconee in middle Georgia, Cofitachiqui in South Carolina, Coosa in Tennessee, northwestern Georgia and northeastern Alabama, and Tascaluza in central Alabama. Unfortunately, from an archaeological point of view, the DeSoto expedition did not pass through the lower Chattahoochee River Valley, and it is not known to which chiefdom the Mississippian settlements in the Valley belonged.

However, as stated, the archaeological record from this era is extensive along the Chattahoochee on both banks of the river. The principal Mississippian sites in the Valley include, on the Georgia side, the late stages of Kolomoki and Mandeville; Rood's Landing and Singer-Moye in Stewart County; the Pataula Creek Junction site and Cemochechobee in Clay County; Bull Creek near Columbus; and Drag Nasty Creek, Graces Bend, and the Cool Branch site, all near Fort Gaines. In Alabama we have Omussee Creek and Spann's Landing in Houston County; the Reeves site, Lampley Mound, and Lynn's Fish Pond, all near Eufaula; and Abercrombie mound in Russell County. Many Mississippian sites in the Chattahoochee River Valley have been covered by impoundment waters, worn down by farming, or washed away by high water. For example, the Reeves site, Lampley Mound, and Lynn's Fish Pond are all covered by Lake Walter F. George. The western edge of Cemochechobee is eroding into the lake. Mandeville is now under water. There were once large platform mounds at Kyle's (Woolfolk's) Bend at what became the Columbus city dump. A steamboat landing near the latter was known as "Mound Landing" throughout the 19th Century, but the earthen heap was washed into the river around 1900.

It is important to realize that many, if not most, of these sites have yielded artifacts--copper ornaments and headdresses, pole spud maces, human and animal effigy vessels bearing the barred oval design--associated with the Southeastern Ceremonial Complex. Therefore, most probably the Mississippian people of the Chattahoochee River Valley participated in some sort of pre-Columbian, pan-Indian consciousness in America, the exact nature of which is as yet poorly understood. Clearly, however, the early people of the Valley were more articulated with the outside world than we are accustomed to thinking.

Wolf met Terrapin and boasted that he could outrun him. Terrapin said, "I am fast," and Wolf said, "I am fast, too." Then Terrapin said to Wolf, "Let us run a race."

After they had set a day, Terrapin went away and looked for some other terrapin. They had agreed to race across four hills and so Terrapin set one terrapin on each of the hills, but he sat on the last himself. When the time had come, and Wolf had arrived, Terrapin said, "When I whoop I am going to start."

Presently, he whooped and immediately Wolf ran as fast as he could go until he got up on top of one of the hills. When he came there he saw a terrapin climb the next and sit down upon it. He ran on again and when he got to top of that hill, he saw a terrapin climb up on the third hill and sit down. Wolf thought he was beaten so he left and went away. On a later day, when Terrapin and Wolf met, Terrapin said, "You said you did not believe me, but I beat you."

It is told that way.

A Hitchiti Tale

VIII

Rood's, Singer-Moye, Cemochechobee

Archaeological excavations at Mississippian sites in the Valley illustrate just how advanced was the Indian civilization of the time. They also furnish concrete examples of the objects and practices of daily life. While most of the sites contain only one or two mounds, several--Rood's and Singer-Moye, for example--are magnificent complexes with extensive grounds and numerous large mounds.

The Rood's site, which covers more than fifteen acres, is located on the north bank of the creek of that name, a favorite of modern-day bass fisherman. It consists of eight, possibly nine mounds, five of which are situated around a large open area (now overgrown) which may once have been a plaza. The mounds and village area are actually on a peninsula formed by Rood's Creek on the south and by another, smaller creek on the west. Two moats and a palisade once enclosed the site, connecting the two creeks, providing strong fortification against enemies.

Joseph R. Caldwell did a partial excavation of Rood's in 1955 under the sponsorship of the Columbus Museum. His excavation revealed at least three flat-topped platform mounds, all of which had once had houses or other structures on their summits. All of the mounds appeared to have multiple summits, having received new caps of clay and earth at successive periods during the long occupation of the Rood's site. This capping appears to have been ceremonial in nature, possibly attendant to the deliberate firing and destruction of the buildings or structures found on the various summits within the mounds. As previously mentioned, authorities believe such ritual firings were connected with rites of purification and renewal.

Mound A had two ramps leading to its summit, which was

twenty-five feet high. A low rampart of clay ran around the summit, an area of approximately a quarter-acre. There were a number of burned buildings on the mound's top. All of the structures showed construction techniques found among Indians in the Valley in historic times. These included four large vertical central posts supporting roof stringers, a central fire hearth, and smaller pine posts forming an outside wall that was finished with horizontal cane strips heavily daubed with clay. At least one structure had been covered with a low mound of earth after it was burned.

Caldwell was unable to determine whether these structures were secular or sacred in nature--that is, whether they represented domiciles, council houses, or buildings used for religious purposes. However, numerous potsherds and scattered animal bones indicated that some of the buildings served as residences at least part of the time.

An adult male and a six-year-old child were found buried in the south corner of the mound, each lying on his back, fully extended, and with the left leg crossed over the right. Small ceramic and stone discs, fragments of pottery elbow pipes, three triangular flint projectile points, some charred oak acorns and corncobs, and several fossilized shark's teeth were found among the summit debris. A carefully modeled, life-sized pottery phallus was unearthed near the remains of one of the buildings. It may have been used in fertility rites.

Mound B also had a structure on its summit, numerous potsherds scattered about, and a small pit. The pit contained several sherds of pottery, one with rim decoration--called an "adorno" by archaeologists--representing a pelican, calcined bone, charcoal, charred acorns, a fire-cracked stone and a charred bean of what was probably *Stewartia malachodendron*, a member of the tea family. An infant was found buried in the lower level of this mound, which also yielded fragments of pottery elbow pipes, burned wall plaster, a large pottery vessel with six loop handles, and several shard discs.

Two other mounds at the site were examined briefly but

revealed little in the way of unusual artifacts.   More recent investigations have revealed that Mound E, a large platform mound near the center of the complex, is almost exactly square and is oriented toward the four cardinal directions, a recurring theme, as we shall see, in public architecture among the natives of the Chattahoochee River Valley.

Some of the pottery at Rood's was quite expertly made and beautifully decorated in what archaeologists call Lamar Complicated Stamped, that is, with whorling figure-eight designs and circles within circles.   Other pottery fragments recovered from the deepest, hence earliest levels, at Rood's are so different from pottery found elsewhere in Georgia from the same time period that Caldwell thought them the product of a new, invading people from the West.   He postulated that the original Mississippian settlement at Rood's had been established by invaders who dislodged the local inhabitants, driving them south and east.   This early pottery from Rood's is very similar to that found at Macon and at Hiwassee Island in eastern Tennessee.   The more recent pottery, such as that recovered from the summit of Mound A, appears related to the Fort Walton culture of north Florida.

Singer-Moye

Singer-Moye is a magnificent Mississippian site on Pataula Creek about 29 miles from its confluence with the Chattahoochee and 17.5 miles east-southeast of Rood's.   Located deep within a pine and hardwood forest, which includes towering walnut and hickory trees, the site covers more than 32 acres and contains six platform mounds, a plaza and village area, and a square earth lodge. Singer-Moye, which is owned by the Columbus Museum, has been repeatedly studied since the late 1960s under the direction of museum archaeologist Frank Schnell.

Mound A, the largest mound at Singer-Moye, is approximately 45 feet high and has ramps leading to the summit on its northeast and southwest sides. The corners of the mound are precisely aligned with the cardinal directions. Because of the southward slope of the land on the site, the south side of Mound A is about six feet higher than the north side. A large building, some 1,300 square feet in area, was found on the summit. It had eight major roof supports and a fireplace similar to ones found at Cemochechobee. As was the case with the structures on the summit of the mounds at Rood's, the building had been burned. It had then been capped with clay in a manner reminiscent of one of the structures atop Mound A at Rood's. A radio-carbon dating of the remains of one of the roof supports from Mound A at Singer-Moye yielded a date of A.D. 1390 plus or minus 60 years.

The summit of Mound D at the site was exposed to reveal six large fire pits similar to fire pits found at the Yon site on the Upper Apalachicola River and on Mound B at Cemochechobee. The pits appear too close together to have been in separate structures and too far apart to have been in one large structure. Their use may have been purely ceremonial in nature.

But perhaps the most interesting feature of the Singer-Moye complex is an earthen lodge, approximately 575 square feet in area, discovered in the northwest portion of the site. Although it has been only partially excavated to date, its architecture resembles an earth lodge uncovered at Brown's Mount near Macon. Four central vertical poles supported a roof composed of slanting beams covered with earth. There was a central fireplace with possibly a smoke hole in the roof above. Charcoal recovered from a refuse pit inside the earthlodge yielded a radio-carbon date of A.D. 1275 plus or minus 80 years.

Cemochechobee

Although much smaller than Rood's and Singer-Moye, Cemochechobee (pronounced sa mo che cho bee) is one of the most carefully investigated pre-historic sites in the entire Chattahoochee River Valley. As such, it serves as a window on the past and affords a detailed view of life in the Valley during Mississippian times.

Cemochechobee, located in Clay County, Georgia, was

excavated in 1976-1978 by a team led by archaeologist Frank Schnell under the sponsorship of the Columbus Museum. It is one of several interrelated sites in the Valley, that includes Spann's Landing and Cool Branch. Along with Rood's and Singer-Moye, these Mississippian complexes flourished on the Chattahoochee River from around 900 to 1400, a local cultural manifestation archaeologists call the "Rood Phase." To the south on the Apalachicola River, to the east in the Macon Plateau area, to the west at Bessemer, Alabama, and in the Tennessee-Cumberland region to the north were other contemporaneous Mississippian mound centers with which the Rood Phase people of the Valley appear to have had cultural and trade relations.

There are three mounds (A,B and C) at Cemochechobee, set on a north-south axis on the river bank and so close together that mounds A and B merge. Only Mounds A and B were completely excavated. Archaeologists refer to the mound area as the "nuclear zone." A large village, covering more than 150 acres, surrounded the mounds to the east in Mississippian times, but much of the village area has been destroyed or disturbed by modern-day construction. Activity within the nuclear zone at Cemochechobee was primarily ceremonial or civic in nature. The structures atop the mounds included charnel houses and residences that probably housed Cemochechobee's elite leaders--perhaps the chief administrator, some of his clan, and the head shaman or priest. Due to the orientation of the mounds, the buildings or structures on top of them faced the rising summer sun, one of several reasons archaeologists and anthropologists think the religion of Mississippian people, like the religion of the Woodland or burial mound people before them, was based on sun worship.

Premound Stage
Cemochechobee was settled shortly after 900. Even in the earliest, premound stage, the nuclear zone seems to have been divided into northern and southern precincts, initially by a low wall, a functional division that persisted throughout

Cemochechobee's history.   The northern precinct of the premound stage contained a cluster of five features.   Among these were two small ground pits, one of which contained an interesting assortment of artifacts, a post hole to accommodate a vertical wooden pillar some 23 inches in diameter, two ground pits containing what are apparently hearth ashes, and a section of a wall trench that has been radio-carbon dated to 970, plus or minus 55 years.   The wooden post may be an early example of an Indian *chunk* or game pole, or it may be a slave post, both of which occurred in historic Indian villages along the Chattahoochee.

One of the pits contained a fragmentary piece of sandstone, several lumps of white micaceous clay, several potsherds, a lump of charcoal, and what appears to be a fragment of a soft-fired clay figure.   The excavators of the site think this collection might be a sort of cultural time capsule, a deliberately buried sample of the raw materials used for some unknown purpose, most likely ritualistic, by the Cemochechobee elite.   The figurine suggests ceremonial or ritual use, possibly in fertility rites.

In the next stage of construction, all the earlier features were removed but not burned.   A puddled, outdoor clay hearth appears where the dual partition was located.   Most likely, a ceremonial fire was kept burning in this hearth, perhaps perpetually.

An adult male, fully extended on his back, was found buried in close association with the clay hearth.   Charred logs or bark strips covered the body, which showed evidence of torture and was buried without its feet.   A long greenstone pole spud, probably a symbol of rank and definitely a part of Southeastern Ceremonial Complex paraphernalia, was in the skeleton's right hand.   A fragment of copper was found on the right shoulder.

Ten feet north of the clay hearth were indications of a wall of a large ceremonial compound or ball ground, measuring more than 70 feet in length and nearly 40 in width. The compound was enclosed by a vertical log wall with openings in its northern and southern ends. Pieces of *chunkee* stones, with which historic Indians of the Valley played a favorite game, were found within the compound area. In historic times, such areas were used for dances and ceremonies in addition to games.

Directly opposite the southern end of the compound were two buildings, both of which appear to have been associated with mortuary practices. One of these structures was a charnel house constructed mainly of red cedar. Thirteen individuals, male and female, were found buried in the floor of this structure. Four of these were children or adolescents. Nine of the individuals, all adults, were buried in deep tombs. Some of the skeletons were disarticulated or rearticulated, suggesting that the bones had been stripped of flesh and stored in the building prior to burial. Curiously, the teeth of many of the dead were stained red with a vegetable dye, and many of the skeletons showed signs of platycnemia, a stress-related developmental disorder. Included among the grave goods found with these nine burials were shell ear ornaments, marine bead necklaces, ceramic beakers and effigy bowls, a so-called Nunnally Incised bottle, various shards of "killed" pottery-- pottery which had been ritually broken--greenstone celts, and a copper headdress with adornments in the shape of arrowheads. Three children and one adolescent were buried in pits in the charnel house floor. Artifacts recovered from these burials include shell beads, a large beaver adorno broken from a pot, and pebble hammerstones. Archaeologists think the 13 burials may represent an elite kinship group, perhaps that of a single clan, relations of a Cemochechobee chief or Big Man.

In the next premound stage at Cemochechobee, a large domestic structure, more than 20 feet long and 15 feet wide, replaces the walled compound or ball ground. Evidence indicates that this was the residence of the elite kinship group whose members were interred in the floor of the charnel house. Numerous fragments of animal and fish bones and the remains of plant foods were recovered from the floor of the structure. What appears to be the remains of a kit to make columnar beads from marine shells was found among the debris on the floor. It may be that the elite rulers of Cemochechobee at this stage controlled the manufacture and trade of such beads. A number of refuse pits were found around the house. One contained a fragment of a human effigy bottle cleverly designed so that the individual's mouth is the opening.

Ultimately, the residential structure was dismantled and replaced with a series of large circular buildings, one of which was more than 25 feet in diameter. These structures were almost identical to circular houses found in premound stages at Mississippian complexes at Hiwassee Island in Tennessee and at Bessemer, Alabama. They were also quite similar to historic Creek *Chokofulgi* or council houses.

Mound Construction

At about the time the circular buildings were erected at Cemochechobee, the old mortuary buildings were dismantled and covered with yellow sand--the first evidence of mound building at the site. An adult male was found buried beneath the mound cap, which is the earliest stage of Mound A. Wood charcoal, from cedar, recovered from a hearth on top of the newly built mound has been radio-carbon-dated to 940 plus or minus 55 years.

Shortly after this initial attempt at mound building, a mantle of sand and clay was laid over the top and sides of Mound A, making it approximately three feet high, 63 feet long and 59 feet wide--very nearly square. Although no structural remains were found on top of Mound A from this stage of its construction, numerous killed   pottery vessels were collected from   the surface.

In the next stage, Mound A's height was roughly doubled. Seventeen poorly preserved burials were found in association with this new covering. The excavators believe these burials, which included articulated and disarticulated skeletons of males and females of varying ages, represent the contents of a charnel house that was emptied at the time the new mantle of clay and sand was added. Numerous grave goods were found among the burials, including a shell ear pin, the remains of two wooden or gourd rattles, dog effigy and human effigy bottles bearing the barred oval or ogee symbol of the Southeastern Ceremonial Complex, a marine shell necklace, a fragment of mica, two greenstone celts, a marine shell dipper, and many pieces of killed pottery vessels. The human effigy bottle is of an individual with his hair in a bun, with pierced ears and wearing a cloak or cape. The cloak is covered with the barred oval symbol.

The circumstances of the burials lead archaeologists to believe that the dead were members of the same kinship group or chief clan as the 13 earlier burials in the premound stage. No evidence of any structure was found on the top of Mound A from this period.

Meanwhile, Mound B, adjacent to Mound A, was begun. Shortly after the last of the circular houses was dismantled, it was covered with a mantle of sand and raised to a height of approximately three feet. In its initial stage, Mound B was 32 feet long and 28 feet wide. On the mound's east side there was a small rectangular projection, containing a series of log steps, that might have been a speaker's platform. A house, built of upright timbers and probably covered with bark or thatch, was situated on the summit. This structure faced east and is considered by Cemochechobee's excavators to have been an elite domicile. It had a central hearth. The floor of the house was littered with animal bones, shards, and mussel shells. A small greenstone celt and an unusual greenstone awl or pin were recovered from the debris on the floor.

Another structure, poorly defined, was discovered in the northwestern portion of Mound B. A small child was buried beneath the floor of this structure, which also contained a pit that yielded three copper discs, a flattened copper cone, and some sheet copper.

In the next stage, Mound B was enlarged to the east and another residential building was added. The earlier house was dismantled and covered with debris-laden earth, raising the mound to a height of about four feet. Then, an undetermined number of years later, the second building was dismantled and the mound was completely covered with a new mantle of yellow-orange, sandy clay. After a lapse of many years, the entire mound was again covered with earth, this time a thin, gray, ashy sand. The mound was now more than four feet high, 54 feet long, and 47 feet wide. What appears to have been a small altar or dais was found on the top of this stage of Mound B. Near the altar were the remains of a human skull, possibly a war trophy.

Also located on Mound B at this stage was a large circular building, 24 feet in diameter, with a sunken floor. It was constructed of poles driven in the ground, bent over, and secured around a central smoke hole. It was probably covered with bark shingles or thatch. A large storage pit was dug into the floor of this structure.

Human effigy bottle

Next came another mantle of sandy clay. A ramp was built on the eastern flank of the mound and six steps were modeled into its slope. Six fire pits, reminiscent of those found atop Mound E at Singer-Moye, were discovered on Mound B at this stage. Some years later another mantle was added, considerably enlarging the mound and increasing its height to well over six feet. The earlier ramp was modified and flanked by vertical posts. In his account of the DeSoto expedition, Garcilaso de la Vega describes a similar ramp the Spaniards saw at Osachile in 1540.

The remains of a nearly square building were found on the top of this stage. It was built of pine posts sunk in a wall trench. It sides were wattle and daub. Both stick and split cane wattle were used, and the bright orange clay daub still disclosed, after the passage of a thousand years, imprints of the human fingers that had pressed and smoothed it into place. This building, which included a storage pit in the floor and an auxiliary chamber on its western side, had been burned. The lower half of a human clay figure, seated in the lotus position, was found in the burned rubble, as were a ceramic pipe and several vessels and jars. The excavators think the building was an elite domicile that was used periodically for religious functions and civic councils. The auxiliary chamber may have been used to store sacred vessels and objects.

At approximately this point in Cemochechobee's history, Mound A received two final mantles of earth, the first of clay and the last of sand. The clay used in these caps was evidently brought in basketful by basketful. Killed or ritually destroyed pottery was found on the summit of Mound A from this stage, but there is no evidence of any structures having been present. Apparently, after the final sand mantle was added, Mound A was simply abandoned forever.

Mound B, on the other hand, received four more mantles, resulting in the enlargement of the northern portion of the mound. In the process the ramp on the mound's eastern flank was covered and the boundary between Mound A and Mound B became less distinct. At one point, three buildings stood on Mound B's summit at the same time. One was probably an elite domicile, another a smaller version of a council house or *chokofa*, and the third of an unknown type. This latter structure contained a crescent-shaped dais or altar. All three buildings were dismantled before the final coverings of clay and sand were placed over the mound. In its final form, Mound B was approximately eight feet high, 92 feet long, and 78 feet wide.

Clearly, the intentional firing or dismantling of the structures atop the mounds, the deliberate covering of the remains of such structures with clay and sand, and the serial capping of the mounds themselves over a period of several hundred years reveal a persistent mound-oriented ceremonialism among the people of Cemochechobee. The question is, of course, to what purpose? Why did the people of Cemochechobee initially bury their elite leaders in mounds, often with valuable grave goods and caches of killed pottery? What purpose did the mounds serve? And why were certain buildings erected atop the mounds and then periodically destroyed and covered with earth? And most puzzlingly, why were the mounds irregularly capped with layers of clay and sand? The excavations at Cemochechobee and at dozens of other Mississippian sites in the Southeast point toward the answers to at least some of these questions.

The interment of selected individuals with status grave goods indicates that the burials at Cemochechobee represent a single kinship or clan unit, probably that of a Big Man or leader who had established dominance over the people. Initially, at least, Big Men must have established their dominance through a combination of physical strength, courage, and cunning. It should be remembered that prowess in war and the hunt were among the most prized attributes of a people whose very life depended upon their ability to defend themselves and secure game for the pot. Eventually, the prestige of the Big Man became associated with his family or clan, which came to be regarded as an elite kinship group. Subsequent Big Men were selected only from that particular clan. In other words, elite status became inherited rather than earned.

At least some of the ceremonies connected with the mounds must have had the purpose of simultaneously honoring Cemochechobee's chief or his clan and reinforcing civilian authority. In fact, such periodic, massive civic projects as mound building undoubtedly served to unify the people and ratify the authority of the current leadership. The fact that they were undertaken at all indicates a high degree of cultural integration and social discipline among the people.

The mounds appear to have had a non-secular or religious function as well. This is particularly evident in the fact that Mound B contains only one burial, and that the Mound A burials are largely restricted to two sequences. Moreover, the thin mantles that were repeatedly laid over the mounds, the large number of hearths devoid of animal or plant remains, and the ash lenses covering the mound tops appear to have no secular explanation. It is indicated, too, in the artifacts recovered from some of the pits, including the ceramic figurine, the effigy vessels with symbols of the Southeastern Ceremonial Complex, the killed pottery, and in the orientation of the structures--and most of the burials--to the cardinal directions. Classically, the repeated covering of mounds and the rites accompanying such coverings have been interpreted as indicative of community rites of intensification, renewal, and rebirth.   Such ceremonies indicate preoccupation with the dead or with particular tribal ancestors. The dead, old structures and various sacred objects are buried, ceremonially burned, dismantled, or killed--sacrificed--to appease the evil spirits, cleanse the grounds, and absolve the people of their transgressions. We will encounter this idea in a much more specific context in the aforementioned *Poskeeta* or Green Corn Ceremony of the later Indians of the Valley.

Affairs of Plain Living

So much for the social and religious aspects of the daily life of the people of Cemochechobee. What did the excavations at the site teach us about the more mundane affairs of everyday living? The answer is, a great deal.

For example, we know from bones recovered from domestic environments at Cemochechobee that the favorite animal food of the people was the white-tailed deer. They also ate gray and fox squirrels, cottontail rabbits, and wild turkey. Fish, especially catfish, were an important part of their

Ethlo, *squirrel*

diet. So were turtles and possibly passenger pigeons. Other animals eaten by the people of Cemochechobee included the opossum, the dog or wolf, mountain lion or panther, bobcat, and skunk. For reasons not clearly understood, except for turkeys and pigeons, birds do not appear to have constituted a significant portion of the people's diet. Perhaps fragile bird bones perished quickly in the harsh environment. The Indians may also have been loath to kill birds because they had observed that the creatures ate mosquitoes and other insect pests.

Botanical remains recovered from the site include oak acorns and hickory nuts, two staples of the food supply of Valley Indians since at least early Woodland times. Remains of corn cobs and numerous corn kernels were found. Quite a number of persimmon seeds were present. Persimmons were the favorite fruit of Valley Indians, who ate them raw or cooked them in stews or baked them into a dense bread. Although their numbers were too small to indicate significant use, seeds from the passionflower *(Passiflora incarnata)* and unidentified species of goosefoot *(Chenopodium)* and greenbrier *(Smilax)* were recovered. The seeds of various chenopods are highly nutritious and can be eaten cooked or pounded into a flour. Many parts of greenbriers are edible, and the large roots were a favorite food of the historic Creeks in the Valley. The passionflower or maypop is still occasionally eaten as a seasonal fruit in these parts.

We know, too, from the Cemochechobee dig that the favorite wood for cooking fires was oak. Pine was undoubtedly used to help start fires and perhaps even to cook with when a pot was used. For broiling meat over an open flame, oak was preferred (of the wood charcoal recovered from Cemochechobee, 47.1 percent was oak). Hickory was also used to broil meat.

The people cooked in pots tempered with grit and shell, which produced a sturdy vessel. Many types and shapes of ceramic vessels were in use at Cemochechobee during the Mississippian Period. These include water bottles, plain and incised, human effigy bottles, large and small bowls, including many with handles and spouts, and numerous beakers or cups. Some bowl rims were decorated with adornos representing animals, including beavers, ducks, owls, and hawks or eagles. Many decorative motifs were used on pottery, ranging from punctuated geometric patterns to incised chevrons, circles or scrolls, and cross-hatching.

Tobacco

Ceramic elbow pipe bowls were also recovered from the site, many of which had been decorated with parallel lines that imitate binding. The pipe rims frequently bear a punctuated design thought to represent the weeping eye design of the Southeastern Ceremonial Complex. Similar pipes have been found at Hiwassee Island in north Georgia, at Etowah, and in north Florida.

Although no tobacco was recovered at Cemochechobee, the Indians were probably growing and smoking *Nicotiana rustica* or Indian tobacco (called by the Creeks "the ancient peoples' tobacco"). Sometimes dried leaves of the sweetgum or smooth sumac *(Rhus glabra)* were mixed with the tobacco, producing a milder blend. We know that Southern Indians of the 16th century smoked tobacco habitually, especially before and sometimes during any important occasion. The practice was probably of considerable antiquity, and most certainly went back as far as the Mississippian Period. Interestingly, very early after white contact the French observed the Natchez Indians in what is now Mississippi ingesting concentrated pellets of tobacco to stupify themselves before being ceremonially strangled to accompany their leader to the other world. This is but one example of what was an extensive native American pharmacopoeia based on wild plants, a subject which we will treat in some detail in a later chapter.

Among other interesting objects found at Cemochechobee were 10 small clay discs, thought to be gambling tokens of some sort. The historic Indians of the Valley were passionate gamblers who enjoyed games and wagers of all sorts. Perhaps their Mississippian ancestors did as well.

Cemochechobee teaches us a great deal about the life of Valley Indians during the Mississippian times, but for every question it answers, it raises another. Why was the first individual to be buried in the premound stage of Mound A interred without his feet? What explains the red stain on the teeth of so many of the individuals buried in the mounds? Were the people of Cemochechobee ingesting some sort of fruit, seed, or root that stained their teeth red? If so, what was it? And why did so many of the skeletons reveal platycnemia, a developmental abnormality related to stress? And finally, of course, what happened to the people of Cemochechobee? Why did they abandon the mounds some time around 1400? Were they wiped out by disease, driven away by a more powerful group, or did they suffer some terrible hidden catastrophe?

Perhaps we will never know the answers to all these questions, questions which could be asked of all the Mississippian sites in the Chattahoochee River Valley and elsewhere across America.   Although some of the platform mound complexes in Georgia and Alabama were functioning as ceremonial centers right up until 1540 when Hernando de Soto and his throng of conquistadors marched through the Southeast, several of those in the Valley--Singer-Moye and Cemochechobee among them--appear to have been abandoned at least a century before De Soto. In sum, many authorities now think European and African diseases--smallpox, whooping cough, measles, influenza--introduced by the dozens of voyages of exploration to America and the Caribbean in the late 15th and early 16th centuries, may have preceded the De Soto expedition by a sort of contact diffusion, decimating the people of the temple mound culture throughout the Southeast, including here in the Chattahoochee River Valley. Perhaps the Norsemen who landed on Nova Scotia in the 13th and 14th centuries brought diseases with them that gradually spread through the Eastern United States, reaching the Southeast and the Chattahoochee River Valley in the later 1300s. Other authorities believe that simply the appearance of the Europeans, mounted on huge beasts which the Indians had never seen, and armed with terrible weapons that spoke in flame and thunder and struck down a man three hundred yards away, sent a shock wave through the platform mound people, discrediting their religious and social organization and destroying the mythic underpinnings of their civilization, a blow from which they never recovered.

A chief sent his son on a message to another chief and delivered to him a vessel as the emblem of his authority.

The son stopped to play with some boys who were throwing stones into the water. The chief's son threw his vessel upon the water and it sank. He was frightened. He was afraid to go to the neighboring chief without the vessel, and he did not like to return home and tell his father of the loss. He jumped into the stream and, reaching the spot where the vessel had sunk, he dived into the water. His playmates waited a long time for him, but he did not reappear. They returned and reported his death.

When the chief's son was beneath the surface of the stream the Tie-snakes seized him and bore him to a cave and said to him: "Ascend yonder platform." He looked and saw seated on the platform the king of the Tie-snakes. The platform was a mass of living Tie-snakes. He approached the platform and lifted his foot to ascend, but the platform ascended as he lifted his foot. Again he tried, with the same result. The third time he tried in vain. The Tie-snakes said, "Ascend."

He lifted his foot the fourth time and succeeded in ascending the platform and the king invited him to sit by his side. Then the king said to him:

"See yonder feather; it is yours," pointing to a plume in the corner of the cave. He approached the plume and extended his hand to seize it, but it eluded his grasp. Three times he made the attempt and three times it escaped him. On the fourth attempt he obtained it.

"Yonder tomahawk is yours," said the Tie-snakes' king.

He went to the place where the tomahawk was sticking and reached out his hand to take it, but in vain. It rose of itself every time he raised his hand. He tried four times and on the fourth trial it remained still and he succeeded in taking it.

The king said: "You can return to your father after three days. When he asks where you have been, reply: 'I know what I know,' but on no account tell him what you do know. When he needs my aid, walk toward the east and bow three times to the rising sun and I will be there to help him."

After three days the Tie-snake carried him to the spot where he had dived into the stream, lifted him to the surface of the water, and placed his lost vessel in his hand. He swam to the bank and returned to his father, who was mourning him as dead. His father rejoiced over his son's wonderful restoration.

He informed his father of the Tie-snake king and his message of proffered aid. Not long afterwards his father was attacked by his enemies. He said to his son: "You understand what the king of the Tie-snakes said. Go and seek his aid."

The son put the plume on his head, took the tomahawk, went toward the east, and bowed three times to the rising sun.

The king of the Tie-snakes stood before him.

"What do you wish?" he said.

"My father needs your aid."

"Go and tell him not to fear. They will attack him, but they shall not harm him or his people. In the morning all will be well."

The son returned to his father and delivered the message of the king of the Tie-snakes.

The enemy came and attacked his town, but no one was harmed. Night came. In the morning they beheld their enemies each held fast in the folds of a tie-snake, and so all were captured and the chief made peace with his foes.

A Creek Tale

IX

Migration and Origin Tales

When the first Europeans-- Spanish soldiers, civil authorities, and perhaps a few priests--penetrated the wilderness of the Chattahoochee River Valley in the first half of the 17th century, they found a varied group of red-skinned people living along its banks from the Fall Line south all the way to the river's confluence with the Flint and Apalachicola. Except for the huge mounds in and around

the towns, many overgrown with trees and underbrush, there was almost no visible evidence on the Chattahoochee of the Mississippian civilization that had flourished there from 900 A.D. to sometime around 1500. The Indians the Europeans met- -tall, well-formed warriors with gleaming, black locusts bows, and petite women with numerous offspring--seemed to have no knowledge of the Mississippian Period. They told the Spanish and other early Europeans that the mounds had been built by "the ancient people."

Initially, at least, the Indians the Spanish met in the Valley were not very communicative. The men were proud in bearing, reserved in speech, and cautious, it appeared, almost by nature. Beyond the fact that they had numerous towns on both sides of the river and seemed to defer to the headman of the village of Coweta, whom they called *Miko thluko*--"Big Leader" or "Chief Headman," the Indians offered little information about themselves. However, some of them invited the Spaniards into their towns and asked them to take a seat in one of four cabins arranged in a square, each open on the side facing inward toward a fire that was kept burning in the center of the yard. The headman or *miko* offered them a pipe of native tobacco to smoke and followed this with a black, coffee-like drink the Indians called *a-cee*. After smoking the pipe of peace and drinking prodigious quantities of *a-cee*, which the white men dubbed "the black drink," the Indians were more inclined to talk. They seemed principally interested in trade and offered deer hides and other pelts in exchange for European goods, particularly for steel hatchets, knives, clothing, and guns. The Spanish offered them everything but guns, told them they would have to swear allegiance to the Spanish crown, and then sent in priests to convert them to Christianity. The Indians explained, albeit reluctantly, that they already knew of the One Above, whom they called *Hisagita immisee*, "Master of Breath." When the priests persisted and even erected a cross in the town of Sabacola El Grande in what is now Barbour County, Alabama, in 1679, *Miko thluko* of Coweta ordered them driven out.

English traders soon followed the Spanish into the Valley. By the middle of the 1680s, English traders were at the Fall Line where Columbus and Phenix City are now located. From there they gradually pushed their way to the Indian towns below the Fall Line and westward to the towns on the Coosa and the Tallapoosa Rivers in what is now Alabama. The traders, who included Scotsmen and Irishmen as well as the English, had no interest in converting the Indians to anything. And they were willing to trade them guns, shot, and powder for deer skins and other animal hides. The Indians preferred English guns to the Spanish Catholicism, and although they flirted with the Spanish-- and occasionally the French--from time to time thereafter, they usually remained loyal to the English. Gradually, as the two people got to know each other better, the Indians began to reveal more of themselves.

People of One Fire

They said they were "people of one fire" and lived in many towns on the Chattahoochee, Coosa, and Tallapoosa Rivers. They named Tukabahchee and Abihka as principal towns on the Coosa and Tallapoosa. Other important towns on those rivers-- the traders soon learned to call them "Upper Towns" to distinguish them from the "Lower Towns" on the Chattahoochee- -were Coosa itself, Talladega, Hilibi, Atasi, Tulsa, Okfuskee, and Tuskegee. On the Chattahoochee among the Lower Towns, Kawita (Coweta) and Kasihta (Cusseta) were the most important settlements. In fact, both Cusseta and Coweta were called "mother towns" or "foundation towns" and their chiefs or mikos were often leaders of the entire nation. Other important towns on the Chattahoochee included Coweta Tallahassee (Old Coweta), Chiaha, Yuchi, Osochi (Oswichee), Hitchiti, Apalachicola (sometimes called Pallachucola), Sawokli, Oconee, Eufaula Hopai, and Eto-Husse-Wakkes. Many of these large towns had smaller, outlying settlements, some as far east as the Flint River and its western tributaries, some west of the Chattahoochee on its Alabama tributaries.

Around crackling night fires of pine and oak, the Creek headmen and warriors told the traders that while they had no exact knowledge of their origin, they believed themselves to have sprung from the ground somewhere in the West, perhaps from "the navel of the earth," which they placed in the Rocky Mountains. Prompted with a little rum, for which they developed an immediate appetite, they told elaborate tales of their people's peregrinations, complete with encounters with fabulous monsters, magical mountains, and rivers as red as blood. The men of each town, which they called, in the singular, a *tulwa*, seemed to have an origin legend or a migration tale of their own that concerned the residents of that town only. For example, the Tukabahchee believed they had descended from the sky. The Yuchi, a non-Muskogee people, believed themselves to be *Tsoyaha*, "offspring of the sun." The inhabitants of Coosa thought they were descendants of the survivors of a great town that had been swallowed up by a river or destroyed by a great earthquake.

The people of Coweta and Cusseta, who lived on opposite sides of the Chattahoochee just below the Fall Line, had their own versions of these tales.   Some were so long and elaborate the Indians had to refer to a white buffalo robe on which pictographs served to recall specific events in the history of the people.   One of the best-known versions went this way:

Pictographs were mnemonic devices.

"At a certain time, the Earth opened in the West, where its mouth is.   The earth opened and the Cussitaws (Cussetas) came out of its mouth, and settled nearby. But the earth became angry and ate up their children;   therefore,   they moved further west. A part of them, however, turned back, and came again to the same place where they had been, and settled there. The greater number remained behind, because they thought it best to do so.   Their children, nevertheless, were eaten by the Earth, so that, full of dissatisfaction, they journeyed toward the sunrise. They came to a thick, muddy, slimy river (the Mississippi), came there, camped there, rested there, and stayed overnight there.

"The next day, they continued their journey and came, in one day, to a red, bloody river. They lived by this river, and ate of its fishes for two years; but there were low springs there; and it did not please them to remain. They went toward the end of this bloody river and heard a noise as of thunder. They approached to see whence the noise came.   At first, they perceived a red smoke and then a mountain which thundered; and on the mountain, was a sound as of singing. They sent to see what this was; and it was a great fire which blazed upward and made this singing noise.   This mountain they named the King of Mountains.   It thunders to this day; and men are very much afraid of it.

"They here met people of three different Nations. They had taken and saved some of the fire from the mountain; and, at this place, they also obtained a knowledge of herbs and of many other things.

"From the East, a white fire came to them; which, however, they would not use. From Wahalle (the South) came a fire which was blue; neither did they use it. From the West, came a fire which was black; nor would they use it. At last, came a fire from the North, which was red and yellow. This they mingled with the fire they had taken from the mountain; and this is the fire they use today; and this, too, sometimes sings.

"On the mountain was a pole which was very restless and made a noise, nor could anyone say how it could be quieted. At length, they took a motherless child and struck it against the pole and thus killed the child. They then took the pole, and carried it with them when they went to war. It was like a wooden tomahawk, such as they now use, and of the same wood.

"Here, they also found four herbs or roots, which sang and disclosed their virtues: First, *Pasa*, the rattle-snake root; Second, *Miko hoyanidja*, red-root; Third, *Sowatchko*, which grows like wild fennel; and Fourth, *Eschalapootchke*, little tobacco. These herbs, especially the first and third, they use as the best medicine to purify themselves at their Busk. At this Busk, which is held yearly, they fast, and make offerings of the first-fruits.

"Since they learned the virtues of these herbs, their women, at certain times, have a separate fire, and remain apart from the men five, six, and seven days, for the sake of purification. If they neglect this, the power of the herbs would depart; and the women would not be healthy.

"About that time a dispute arose, as to which was the oldest and which should rule; and they agreed, as they were four Nations, they would set up four poles and make them red with clay, which is yellow at first but becomes red by burning. They would then go to war; and whichever Nation should first cover its pole, from top to bottom, with the scalps of its enemies, should be the oldest.

"They all tried, but the Cussitaws covered their pole first and so thickly that it was hidden from sight. Therefore, they were looked upon, by the whole Nation, as the oldest.   The Chickasaws covered their pole next then the Atilamas (Alabamas) but the Obikaws (Abihkas) did not cover their pole higher than the knee.

"At that time, there was a bird of large size, blue in color, with a long tail, and swifter than an eagle, which came every day and killed and ate their people. They made an image in the shape of a woman and placed it in the way of this bird.   The bird carried it off and kept it a long time and then brought it back. They left it alone, hoping it would bring something forth. After a long time, a red rat came forth from it, and they believed the bird was the father of the rat.   They took council with the rat how to destroy its father.   Now the bird had a bow and arrows and the rat gnawed the bowstring, so the bird could not defend itself, and the people killed it.   They called this bird the king of birds.   They think the eagle is also a great king; and they carry its feathers when they go to war or make peace; the red mean war, the white, peace.   If an enemy approaches with white feathers and a white mouth and cries like an eagle, they dare not kill him.

"After this they left that place, and came to a white footpath. The grass and everything around were white; and they plainly perceived that people had been there. They crossed the path and slept near there.   Afterward they turned back to see what sort of path that was and who the people were who had been there, in the belief that it might be better for them to follow that path. They went along it to a creek called *Coloose-hutche*, that is, Coloose-creek, because it was rocky there and smoked.

"They crossed it, going toward the sunrise, and came to a people and a town named Coosaw (Coosa). Here they remained four years. The Coosaws complained that they were preyed upon by a wild beast, which they called a man-eater or lion, which lived in a rock. The Cussitaws said they would try to kill the beast. They dug a pit and stretched over it a net made of hickory bark. They then laid a number of branches, crosswise, so that the lion could not follow them, and, going to the place where he lay, they threw a rattle into his den. The lion rushed forth in great anger and pursued them through the branches. Then they thought it better that one should die rather than all; so they took a motherless child and threw it before the lion as he came near the pit. The lion rushed at it and fell in the pit, over which they threw the net, and killed him with blazing pine wood. His bones, however, they keep to this day; on one side they are red, on the other, blue.

"The lion used to come every seventh day to kill the people; therefore, they remained there seven days after they had killed him. In remembrance of him, when they prepare for war, they fast six days and start on the seventh. If they take his bones with them, they have good fortune.

"After four years they left the Coosaws and came to a river which they called *Nowpawpe*, now *Tallasi-hutche*. There they tarried two years; and, as they had no corn, they lived on roots and fishes, and made bows, pointing the arrows with beaver teeth and flint-stones, and for knives they used split canes. They left this place and came to a creek, called *Watoola-hawka-hutche*, Whooping-creek, so called for the whooping of cranes, a great many being there; they slept there one night. They next came to a river, in which there was a waterfall; this they named the *Owatunka-river*. The next day they reached another river, which they called the *Aphoosa pheeskaw*. The following day they crossed it, and came to a high mountain, where were people who, they believed, were the same who made the white path. They, therefore, made white arrows and shot at them, to see if they were good people. But the people took their white arrows, painted them red, and shot them back. When they showed these to their chief, he said that it was not a good sign; if the arrows returned had been white, they could have gone there and brought food for their children, but as they were red they must not go. Nevertheless, some of them went to see what sort of people they were and found their houses deserted. They also saw a trail which led into the river; and, as they could not see the trail on the opposite bank, they believed that the people had gone into the river and would not again come forth.

"At that place is a mountain, called *Moterell*, which makes a noise like beating on a drum; and they think this people live there. They hear this noise on all sides when they go to war.

"They went along the river, till they came to a waterfall, where they saw great rocks and on the rocks were bows lying; and they believed the people who made the white path had been there.

"They always have, on their journeys, two scouts who go before the main body. These scouts ascended a high mountain and saw a town. They shot white arrows into the town; but the people of the town shot back red arrows. Then the Cussitaws became angry and determined to attack the town, and each one have a house when it was captured.

"They threw stones into the river until they could cross it, and took the town (the people had flattened heads) and killed all but two persons. In pursuing these they found a white dog, which they slew. They followed the two who escaped, until they came again to the white path and saw the smoke of a town and thought that this must be the people they had so long been seeking. This is the place where now the tribe of Palachucolas live, from whom Tomochichi is descended.

"The Cussitaws continued bloody-minded; but the Palachucolas gave them black drink, as a sign of friendship, and said to them: Our hearts are white, and yours must be white, and you must lay down the bloody tomahawk, and show your bodies as a proof that they shall be white. Nevertheless, [they were for the tomahawk;] but the Palachucolas got it by persuasion and buried it under their beds. The Palachucolas likewise gave them white feathers and asked to have a chief in common. Since then

they have always lived together.
"Some settled on
one side of the river,
some on the other.
Those on one side
are called Cussitaws,
those on the other,

Cowetas; yet they are one people, and the principal towns of the Upper and Lower Creeks. Nevertheless, as the Cussitaws first saw the red smoke and the red fire, and make bloody towns, they cannot yet leave their red hearts, which are, however, white on one side and red on the other. They now know that the white path was the best for them."

The traders, and later the American settlers who followed them into the Valley, listened to this story, which seemed half truth and half fiction, noted its imaginative language and repeated use of the numbers four and seven, and wondered at its meaning. Sometimes they heard other versions, for the Indians of both the Upper and Lower towns relished oratory and used almost any occasion as an excuse to deliver a "talk" about their traditions and history. The American Indian agent Benjamin Hawkins, who was often among the Creeks in the Lower towns in the late 18th and early 19th centuries, wrote down a version he heard delivered by *Tussekiah Miko* of Apatai (Upatoi), a branch of Cusseta. Hawkins spoke the Muskogee language and was a very careful observer of the Indians in his charge. What follows is probably as close as we shall ever get to hearing the authentic voice of the native inhabitants of the Chattahoochee River Valley in times past. To get its full effect, you must imagine yourself seated in one of the cabins, or beds, as the Creek called them, in the town square of Apatai or Cusseta at a time near the end of the 18th century.

The occasion is perhaps the great *Poskeeta* or busk, the annual Green Corn Ceremony celebrating the beginning of the Creek new year. *Tussekiah Miko* rises to address his people on the subject of the old beloved path--the venerated tribal traditions

Creek square ground or Chokofa-thluko

as recollected by the elders and handed down generation after generation.   The phonetic spelling of the Creek words and phrases is as Hawkins gave them:

What Tussekiah Miko Said

"There are in the forks of the Red River, west of (the) Mississippi, two mounds of earth.   At this place, the Cussetuh, Cowetuh and Chickasaws found themselves. They were at a loss for fire. Here they were visited by the Hi-you-yul-gee, four men who came from the four corners of the world. One of these people asked the Indians where they would have their fire. They pointed to a place, it was made, and they sat down around it. The Hi-you-yul-gee directed that they should pay particular attention to the fire, that it would preserve them, and let E-sau-ge-tuh E-mis-see (Master of Breath) know their wants. One of these visitors took them and showed them the pas-sau (button snake-root); another showed them Mic-co-ho yon-ejau (probably dwarf grey willow root), then the Au-che-nau (cedar) and Too-loh (sweet bay). ... After this, the four visitors disappeared in a cloud going from whence they came.

"The three towns then appointed their rulers. The Cussetuhs chose Noo-coose-ul-gee (bear clan) to be their Mic-ul-gee (mikos) and the Is-tau-nul-gee to be the E-ne-hau-thluc-ul-gee (people second in command). The Cowetahs chose the Thlotlo-ul-gee (fish clan) to be their Mic-ul-gee.

"After these arrangements, some other Indians came from the west, met them, and had a great wrestle with the three towns. They made ball sticks and played with them, with bows and arrows, and the war club. They fell out, fought, and killed each other. After this warring, the three towns moved eastwardly, and they met the Au-be-cuh at Coosau River. Here they agreed to go to war for four years, against their first enemy. They made shields of buffalo hides, and it was agreed that the warriors of each town should dry and bring forward the scalps of the enemy and pile them. The Aubecuh had a small pile, the Chickasaws were above them, the Cowetuhs above them, and the Cussetuhs above all. The two last towns raised the scalp pole, and do not suffer any other town to raise it. Cussetuh is first in rank.

"After this, they settled the rank of the four towns among themselves. Cussetuh called Au-be-cuh and Chickasaw younger brothers. The Chickasaw and Aubecuhs called Cussetuh and Cowetuh oldest brothers. Au-be-cuh called Chickasaw elders or people ahead of them. Chickasaws sometimes use the same expression for Aubecuh.

"This being done, they commenced their settlements on Coo-sau and Tal-la-poo-sau, and crossing the falls of the Tallapoosa above Tool-cau-bat-che, they visited the Chat-to-hoche and found a race of people with flatheads  in possession of the mounds in the Cussetuh fields. These people used bows and arrows with strings made of sinews. The great physic makers (Au-lic-chul-gee) sent some rats in the night time which gnawed the strings, and in the morning they attacked and defeated the flats. They crossed the river at the land near the mound and took possession of the country. After this they spread out eastwardly, to O-cheese-hat-che (Ocmulgee River), Ocoonee, O-ge-chee (How-ge-chuh), Chic-Nke-tal-lo-fau-hat-che (Savannah River), called sometimes Sau-va-no-gee, the name for Shaw-a-nee. They met the white people on the seacoast, who drove them back to their present situation."

The Creeks fairly generally agreed on the last point. They, as well as the Yuchi, claimed to have been living along the Savannah River and on the eastern seaboard when the first Europeans were sighted coming ashore from their great ships. For this reason, they said, one of their terms for white people was "people of the ocean foam."

Creek basket with double rim

Two Tie-snakes lived on opposite sides of a river bend, unknown to each other. Rabbit, however, knew that they were both there, so one day he went to one of them and said, "Let us get a grapevine and have a tug of war against each other." The snake agreed and they appointed a time. Then Rabbit went over to the Tie-snake on the other side of the bend and made the same agreement with him.

After that he got a grapevine and at the time appointed carried one end to one snake and the other end across to the other. Marks were set to see which could pull the other across. Then Rabbit stationed himself in the middle and shook the vine, and they began pulling, each thinking that Rabbit was at the other end and they thought he was much stronger than they had taken him to be. Each in turn pulled the other near the mark when the other would drag him back. Finally they went around the bend and discovered each other.

They were angry with Rabbit and made it a rule that he should not have any water, but he turned himself into a speckled fawn and in that shape went down and drank all that he wanted.

A Creek Tale

X

Clan Structure

Most of the native inhabitants of the Valley who greeted the Spanish in the 17th century and who later met the English traders and American settlers who poured into the Valley in the 18th and 19th centuries, spoke some dialect of the great Muskogean Indian language group. They included the Apalachicola, Hitchiti, and Creeks or Muskogulgi, with the latter being by far the most numerous native people on the Chattahoochee, Coosa, and Tallapoosa Rivers. The Yuchi, who spoke an entirely different language, also lived on the Chattahoochee, or moved there shortly after European contact. Two other Muskogean-speaking people, the Alabama and the Koasati, lived along the Alabama and Black Warrior Rivers. West of them were the Choctaw and northwest were the Chickasaw. The Cherokee occupied the area that is now northern Alabama and Georgia and southern Tennessee and North Carolina. Apalachee Indians, whose language was also distantly Muskogean, lived just south of the Chattahoochee-Flint-Apalachicola junction in the area we now call the Florida Panhandle.

Some contemporary scholars think the Muskogulgi were invaders who came into the Chattahoochee River Valley some time around 1500, perhaps as early as 1400--that is, during the time of the collapse of the Mississippian civilization. It has been suggested, for example, that the Creeks were part of the Mississippian chiefdom of Coosa or perhaps of Oconee or Tascaluza, all three of which appear to have collapsed under the impact of war or from epidemics of European or African diseases. The theory is that the Creeks were devastated by their encounters with De Soto and with other Spanish expeditions of the 16th century and retreated into the wilderness to escape. In time, they found their way into the Chattahoochee River Valley, displacing the Hitchiti or Apalachicoli, the original Mississippian people of the Valley, gradually absorbing them into a loose association of native people that eventually included elements of the Alabama, Koasati, Yuchi, Natchez, and even Shawnee. Europeans and Americans have been pleased to call this association the Creek Confederacy, although there is little evidence the Creeks ever did so.

The origin of Valley Indians remains obscure, but Creek migration legends usually mention a strong association with the town of Coosa, whose people may have been a remnant of the great Coosa Province of the Mississippian era. The problem is that European and Indian notions of time do not mix. The Indian origin myths and migration legends may have to do with relatively contemporary events, or they may be a quilt of many different events from widely separated time periods.

Creek Heritage

What is known is that the Creeks and other Indians who met the first Europeans in the Valley behaved as if they had been living here for a long time. They were thoroughly familiar with the Valley's geography, were fully adapted to its climate and seasons, and possessed intimate and detailed knowledge of its plant and animal life. They knew the local game trails and the footpaths of the Valley like the palms of their own hands, and they were capable of traveling hundreds, even thousands, of miles away from home without losing their way. Not only did they travel great distances on their annual winter hunts, but they also had long-established trade relationships with native people all over the Southeast and beyond to the Ohio River Valley and the Rocky Mountains. They hunted and fished in precisely the same manner as the earlier people of the Valley, lived in towns near or actually on the sites of the Woodland and Mississippian people, and maintained religious and social traditions, including veneration of the sun and of fire and the practice of subsistence agriculture based on corn and wild plants, consistent with their predecessors on the Chattahoochee. They ate the same fruits-- persimmons, particularly, and red mulberries--harvested the same nuts and acorns every fall, and lived in houses and villages that often reflected the architecture of earlier inhabitants of the Valley. They also showed immense respect for the tombs of the dead. In other words, the Creeks and other historic native people of the Valley behaved as if they were the rightful inheritors of precious traditions, not the least of which were the essential forest efficiency skills that made them masters of their environment, rather than destroyers of those traditions.

Clan Structure

For a supposedly primitive people, the Creeks had a surprisingly complex and well-organized society. The basic unit of social organization among the Creeks and the other Indians in the Valley was the clan, a tightly knit group of blood relatives whose descent was traced through the mother, that is, matrilineally. Virtually all the Creeks belonged to clans. Not to do so was to be an outcast, beyond the protection of law or custom. Even war captives and slaves sought to be adopted by a clan, which might then protect them against torture or ritual slaughter.

No single factor of Creek society exerted more influence over the daily lives of the Indians than their clan, whose members were required to defend and support each other at all times. Members of the clan looked after each other in health and sickness, shared responsibility for rearing children, cared for the aged, and sheltered the homeless. Clan membership cut across town lines and extended throughout the Creek nation. Thus a member of the Wind clan in Eufaula on the lower Chattahoochee had a kinsman and ally in the Wind clan in Talladega in the Upper towns. Creek custom demanded the extension of hospitality to any visiting clan member from a distant village no matter how impoverished the local clan might be. Members of the same clan were forbidden to intermarry or to engage in sexual relations. The marriage sanction seems to have been rather strictly observed, but there are many amusing stories about violations of the latter rule. When someone did marry within his clan, the Creeks said "he has fallen into his own pot." Allegiance to the clan often superseded allegiance to the Creek nation as a whole.   This custom led to frequent and enduring misunderstandings with Europeans, most of whom insisted that the Indians behave as one "tribe" with one leader or chief.   The Spanish, English, and French (and later, the Anglo-Americans) sought to impose a patriarchal, nation-state system on Indians in order that they might deal with one headman when establishing trade agreements, fixing prices, negotiating financial settlements, signing treaties--that is, extracting land concessions, and fomenting warfare among the Indians.   However, due to the clan structure, the *mikulgi* or chiefs, to use the European term, had very restricted power and almost none whatever within clans other than their own.   Contact with whites gradually increased the power of the Creek *mikulgi*, but until quite late in the history of the Indians of the Chattahoochee no single *miko* or headman had the authority to declare war or sign treaties in the name of all Creeks.

There were many other peculiarities of the clan structure among the Creeks and other Southeastern Indians that perplexed and frustrated Europeans.   Failure to understand the clan structure got many an early white trader killed on the Chattahoochee, and right up until Indian removal began in the 1830s, the clan structure figured in misunderstandings and violence between whites and Creeks and even among the Creeks themselves.

Clan Retaliation

The principal cause of the violence was a rigid law of retaliation, reminiscent of the Old Testament *lex talionis* of an eye for an eye, that applied to all Indian clans.   Should an injury, even an accidental injury, be inflicted on a clan member, the males in the clan were required to exact vengeance in proportion to the extent of the injury--without regard for intent. This law, which was rarely waived, was extended to the elderly, women, and even little children.

If a small boy accidentally put out the eye of a playmate, it was incumbent upon the injured child's clan to put out the eye of the other child. If a man lent his horse to a friend and that friend was thrown and killed, the clan of the dead man was required to kill the man who lent his friend the horse. Should the offending party escape, some other member of the clan would be punished in his place. In the early days, before extended contact with whites, there seems to have been few if any exceptions to his rule of blood vengeance unless absolution was granted during the annual Green Corn Ceremony, which will be discussed later.

Clan Names

A Creek clan was associated with a particular animal or natural phenomenon from which it took its name. Anthropologists have recorded the names of 50 or more Creek clans. The most prominent clans among the Creeks of the Lower towns on the Chattahoochee and the Upper towns on the Coosa and Tallapoosa were:

Wind or *Hotulgulgi*
Bear or *Nokosulgi*
Bird or *Fuswulgi*
Beaver or *Echaswulgi*
Raccoon or *Wotkulgi*
Alligator or *Halpatulgi*
Water moccasin or *Aktayatchulgi*
Deer or *Eachoulgi*
Panther or *Katchulgi*

These nine clans are still powerful among the Creeks in the West, but there is evidence that, at various times during Creek history, other clans—Fish, Polecat, Fox, Potato, Red Paint, to name a few—were of equal importance. We have already seen in *Tussekiah Miko*'s migration legend how the people of Coweta chose the Fish clan as their leaders. Perhaps this refers to the people of Coweta Tallahassee or Old Coweta, whose town was burned by the Spanish in 1685.

Among the clans, the Wind seems to have been the most powerful and important. A woman of the Wind clan was called "grandmother"--*posee*--by the Creeks, and special privileges were extended to Winds. In the old days, the Wind clan supplied many *mikulgi* and second men or *henihulgi* in the Creek towns. We know that in historical times the Wind clan was very important at Cusseta and Coweta. So were the Fish and Potato clans. And other clans, especially the Bear, seem to have been powerful, too.

Clan Councils

The clans were grouped into associations, called "phratries" by scholars, which seem to have been clan councils of some sort. One such phratry was composed of the Wind, Skunk, Fish, Rabbit, Otter, and Turtle. Another included the Bear, Wolf, and Salt clans. These associations were very loose and did not indicate blood kinship. The relationship may have been partially ritualistic or symbolic, as when certain clans in Tukabahchee Town among the Upper Creeks associated themselves with the reputed spiritual powers of the Shawnee and called themselves *Sawanogulgi* or "Shawnee people."

More important to our understanding of the clan structure among the Creeks was a yet larger grouping, called "moities" by anthropologists, that separated all Creek clans into two categories: the *Hathagulgi* or "white people (or) clans" and the *Chelokogulgi* or "people of a different speech."

Although the composition of these categories often varied from town to town, the Wind, Bear, Bird, and Beaver appear to have been most often *Hathagulgi*. The *Chelokogulgi* were usually Raccoon, Water Moccasin, Potato, Alligator, Deer, and Panther. Additionally, the Hitchiti, Alabama, and Yuchi Indians were called *chelokogulgi* because they either spoke a different dialect of Muskogee or, as in the case of the Yuchi, another language altogether.

The *Hathagulgi* were associated with peace and, perhaps, with culture in a broad sense as well. *Chelokogulgi* were the war clans. Anciently, this dual division may have had to do with a caste system within particular towns or associations of *tutk-itka hamkusee*, "people of the same or one fire." However, in historical times the division seems to have been primarily for purposes of social organization. The dual groups balanced each other, thus reflecting what we will soon learn was the essence of Creek religious beliefs. Functionally, they provided a means by which the Creek people might relate to each other in an orderly fashion.

For reasons that are not clearly understood, the *Hathagulgi* (sometimes referred to as *estee alumba*, "people who stick together") were associated with peace, the *estee cheloki*, with war. *Cheloki* does not mean "red," but the *Chelokogulgi* are sometimes called the red clans because, among the Creeks and many other Southeastern Indians, the color red was associated with war.

White Path

The color white, on the other hand, was associated with peace and purity, as well as with that which was old, traditional and, in the modern sense, cultured. It may be that the *Hathagulgi* were originally the inhabitants of the earliest Creek towns--the *tulwa mikulgi* or "chief or principal towns"--which were often called "white towns." Cusseta, as we have seen, was one such white town.

Not all of the old or foundation towns were white towns, however. Tukabahchee on the Tallapoosa River in Alabama was an ancient town placed in the red group. So was Coweta Tallahassee or Old Coweta.

White towns had a specific association with peace and with refuge. No human blood was supposed to be shed in a white town, although we know this custom was violated frequently in historical times. Nevertheless, a murderer or individual fleeing clan revenge might find safety in such towns. During Indian uprisings, white traders, fearing for their lives, often did so.

The early traveler William Bartram relates that Apalachicola

Town (Pallachucola) on the west bank of the Chattahoochee in Russell County, Alabama, was a beloved white town of the nation until several white traders who sought refuge there were put to death. Afterward, it fell into decay and Bartram said the Creeks felt this was because blood had been shed in a holy place. Red towns, on the other hand, were associated with war and specifically with the practice of putting captured enemies to death. Despite this division, it must not be thought that only red towns made war or that white towns remained forever at peace. Neither is the case. The terms are more complex than one might expect and go back to the very earliest origin myths of the Creeks. Red, besides being the color associated with war, was also the color of the earth and was associated with nature and man's natural instincts. White had cultural connotations having to do with the acquisition of knowledge, understanding, and civilization.

In the early part of this century, the anthropologist John R. Swanton compiled a list of white and red towns among Creeks in the West. While time and distance may have altered the categories as known among the Creeks when they lived in this area, Swanton includes among the white towns Cusseta, Apalachicola (Pallachucola), Hitchiti, Sawokli, Okmulgee, Coosa, Tulsa, Lutcapoga, Okfuskee, Abihka, Talladega, Tuskegee, Wiogufki, and Wiwohka. Among the red towns were Coweta, Thleekatcka (Broken Arrow), Chiaha, Osochi, Eufaula, and Tukabahchee.

Although our information on this point is sketchy, it may well be that certain offices in the Creek's social and political structure were once the hereditary right of whites or reds. We know, for example, that a great many "second men" or *henihulgi* came from white clans. Henihas, as they were sometimes called by the traders, were definitely associated with peace among the Indians in this area. Likewise, many *mikulgi* or "chiefs" came from the Bear clan, a white clan. And generally it can be said that red clans supplied the *mikulgi* or headmen of red towns, whites of white towns.

Whereas the individual clans--the Wind, Bear, Beaver, and so on--were categories that operated throughout the Upper and Lower towns, the division into *Hathagulgi* and *Chelokogulgi* had very practical meaning for the Creeks within each town: it separated the men into practice teams for ball play, a sport for which the Indians of this region had a passion.

Away back in the first times God lived on the earth with men and he so arranged it that their hoes, plows, and all other tools worked without being guided. All a man had to do was to tell the hoe or plow where he wanted work done and it was done by the tool itself.

One day God was passing a field where some young men were at work clearing the ground. He asked them:

"What will you plant?" Said they, in derision, "Rocks."

When they returned to the field the next morning it was covered with enormous rocks, so then they could plant nothing.

Another time God passed a house of mourning where a man was lying dead in his coffin. He asked: "Why do you mourn?"

"Our friend is dead," sighed they. "He is not dead," said He, and straightway the dead arose.

Some other young men thought they would deceive their Maker. They put one of their number in a coffin and forthwith began to cry aloud. God asked them: "Why do you cry?"

"Because our friend is dead," they said in pretended sadness.

"If he is dead, he is dead," said He, and when the box was opened, lo, their friend was dead.

Some wicked women passed a field where the hoes and plows were at work and said, "See what a foolish way to work."

"Since you are not contented with my plan, henceforth do the work yourselves," said He, and ever since the women have worked the fields."

A Creek Tale

XI

The Tulwa

Among the Creek's fiercest loyalties was their devotion to their respective towns, which played a role in their daily lives second only to that of their clans. All Creeks belonged to a particular town or *tulwa*. Not to do so was to be a virtual outcast in society. Actually, "town" is an inadequate translation of *tulwa*, a term which meant much more than simply a place of residence to the Creeks. Any sizable *tulwa* encompassed a region, and usually included smaller, satellite villages, farm land, and hunting grounds. So complete was the Creeks' identity with their *tulwa* that they spoke of themselves as being Cowetas, Cussitas, and the like. Tribe may be closer than "town" to the full meaning of *tulwa* to the Creeks.

A Creek *tulwa* might range in size from a few dozen inhabitants to several hundred. As mentioned, the great Lower Creek towns in the Chattahoochee River Valley were Coweta, just below Bull Creek on the Alabama side of the river, and Cusseta, which was located on the Georgia side about where Lawson Field is today. In earlier times, Apalachicola, which was situated below Coweta on the Alabama side in what is now Russell County, was another important Creek *tulwa*. Among the Upper Creeks on the Coosa and Tallapoosa rivers to the west of us, the most important *tulwa* in historic times was Tukabahchee. Just as was the case with their Mississippian predecessors, the Creeks preferred to locate their towns along watercourses, both for convenience and because water played such an important ceremonial role in their lives. A favorite locale was on a high spot just inland on a peninsula jutting out into the Chattahoochee or strung out along a creek upstream from its confluence with the river.

No matter where the Creek town was located or what its size, it was usually organized around a public plaza. Among the main elements of such a plaza was the square ground, sometimes called the *Chokofa-thluko* or "big house," consisting of four partially enclosed rectangular wooden sheds (*tupa*, "bed" or "bench"), oriented to the four cardinal directions. In the summer and in times of good weather, almost all official business of the *tulwa* was transacted in the square, where the town elders and idlers gathered every day to drink *a-cee*, smoke, gossip, trade tall tales, gamble, and discuss the affairs of the town. Important visitors were received in the square, and honored guests usually sat in the *tupa* of the *miko*.

Adjacent to the square was the great town or council house, the *Chokofa*, which was used in the winter and in periods of inclement weather. This was a

Square ground and chokofa *or council house*

circular building large enough to accommodate dozens of persons, with cane benches around the walls and a central fire, usually of dried, split river cane. The *Chokofa* might have a hole in the roof to vent the smoke, but many did not. A small back or side room served as a repository for sacred vessels and ceremonial objects. The *Chokofa* was used for the same purpose as the town square. On winter nights, the building might be used for music or dances, both popular forms of entertainment among the Creeks.

Women ordinarily were not allowed in this male domain unless they were very old and homeless. Then they might be allowed to sleep there in very cold weather. Another exception was for dancing, when women were often invited to come to the *Chokofa* to participate. Women were also discouraged from frequenting the town square except during nightly dances and certain ceremonial occasions. Despite the fact that clan membership among the Creeks was reckoned matrilineally, their society was not a matriarchy. Males dominated almost every aspect of life outside the home. For example, during menstruation, which the Indians looked upon with superstition and fear, women were kept apart and forbidden to touch food, clothing, or any person for fear they would cause spiritual as well as physical defilement. They were also subject to being accused of witchcraft, especially in old age. Any Indian woman identified as a witch could be killed without fear of clan reprisal.

Chunkee Yard

A *chunkee* yard or ball yard, approximately the size of a football field, was in close proximity to the square ground and council house in most Creek towns. Sometimes this area was sunken below the level of the surrounding earth and lined all around with a sort of clay earthwork called a *tudjo*. The Creeks had a passion for all sorts of games of chance, and they were especially fond of rolling a small stone disc, called a *"chunkee* stone" by whites, and throwing a spear or shooting an arrow at the spot where they thought it would come to a stop. Large and small amounts of personal goods were wagered by the participants and the onlookers. The man who came closest to the *chunkee* stone won.

Near the center of the *chunkee* yard was a wooden pole about 30 feet high, to which was attached some such object as a bison's skull or a carved fish or eagle. In historic times, this pole seems to have been chiefly used in friendly and festive games in

which the men and women
vied against each other in
attempts to hit the object
fixed to the top of the pole.
Again, we have seen what
appears to be this pole's
antecedent at several
excavated Mississippian sites
in the Valley.

In the old days, there were two other poles at the far end of
the *chunkee* yard, each about 12 feet high. These were the slave
posts, to which were bound enemies captured in war who were
to be tortured to death or burnt. Some slave poles were topped
with human skulls, according to the early traveler William
Bartram, who passed through the Valley in 1777, and most had
many enemy scalps dangling from them.

Spread out beyond and around the public square, big house
and *chunkee* yard were the dwellings of the *tulwa*'s inhabitants.
The Indians of the Chattahoochee River Valley did not live in
tepees but in airy houses built of wattle and daub or, later, of
wood, and roofed with pine bark or a similar substance. A
typical family arrangement might be two such houses, perhaps
one for summer and one for winter. Sometimes one house
would be used for domestic purposes and the other for storing
grain, deer hides, and roots.

Well-to-do Indians might have four houses arranged rather
like the public square. One house would be used for sleeping,
another for cooking, another for storing corn and for keeping
roots and potatoes dry, and the last for storing deer hides. In
many instances, one of these houses would have a second floor
without walls, making a sort of pavilion where guests were
received and where the family lounged in hot weather.

Usually, the women would have a family vegetable garden
nearby. The communal fields of the *tulwa* were located some
distance away on the rich river bottom lands and along the
creeks.

Sanitation was definitely a problem, and there is evidence that many Creek towns were forced to relocate because of the accumulation of human waste and other refuse. Gathering firewood, which the Indians needed constantly for both their cooking and ceremonial fires, was also a problem. Long occupation of one site would strip the surrounding area of suitable firewood and cause the women to expend much labor and time getting in a daily supply. This is probably one reason the Indians burned split river cane and corn cobs when they could. A town site had to be abandoned when the supply of fire wood was exhausted in its area.

Government

The Creeks were governed by a *miko* or chief and a council of elders consisting of beloved wise men (*estee-achulakulgi*). There is evidence that prior to the coming of the white man, the power of the *miko* was limited, while that of the council of elders was substantial. The leading warriors or *tustunukulgi* of the *tulwa* also had considerable influence over town affairs, primarily, of course, in time of war.

The centralization of authority in a Creek town was complicated by the clan structure. Although individual Creeks might be devoted to their towns and respectful of their *miko* and town council, they were also fiercely loyal to their clan. Thus any direct political or government control over individual Indians by the *miko* was tenuous at best. The *miko* and the council of elders ruled more by persuasion than by absolute authority.

Nevertheless, the *miko* was a relatively powerful figure in any Creek town. As mentioned earlier, it appears that so-called red towns were ruled by *mikulgi* from the red clans, that is, by *Chelokogulgi*, and so-called white towns were ruled by *mikulgi* from the white clans or *Hathagulgi*. Red towns, as we have seen, were anciently identified with war and white towns with peace. Although the practice varied from town to town, *mikulgi* appear to have been elected or appointed by the town elders. They may have been chosen from a particular clan, and we know that heredity played a role in certain cases, but men also rose to the rank of *miko* on the basis of unusual ability in either politics or war.

Despite the male dominance of Indian society, women sometimes rose to the rank of chief or "princess." De Soto and his band encountered such a female ruler in South Carolina in the middle of the 16th century. Mary Musgrove, a Creek woman from Coweta, certainly exerted tremendous influence over the Indian nation in the 18th century. And so-called "beloved women" wielded considerable power and influence among the Indians who inhabited the Chattahoochee River Valley throughout the historic period. Women also served as healers or doctors, a role in which their extensive knowledge of plants was an important element.

Before the coming of the Europeans, the *miko* was associated with peace and was regarded as a civil official. *Mikulgi* had charge of the *Chokofa* and the town square. In historic times they directed all important affairs for the town--or attempted to do so--by oratory and persuasion. They received all foreign visitors, listened to their speeches or talks and replied in kind, entered into negotiations with other towns and tribes, and generally exerted as much influence on public and domestic affairs as their own reputations and leadership ability allowed. Some *mikulgi* became powerful figures, developed local political bases, and extended their influence throughout the Creek nation. Others were content to exert influence in their own *tulwa*.

Layout of Square

Almost all the town's business was transacted in the square, with its four wooden beds oriented in relation to the four cardinal points. Each bed or *tupa* was open on the side facing inward, like a lean-to, and was about 30 to 40 feet in length. It was divided into two or three compartments by a waist-high partition of cane and clay. Several rows of cane benches ran the length of the entire *tupa*, with the rear benches elevated slightly above those in front. The roofs of these structures might be decorated with war emblems, various vegetable medicines, and perhaps the feathers of eagles or of some other bird of prey. Each *tulwa* seems to have had a symbol, usually an animal, bird or fish, which was displayed in the town square. A war pole or *atasa* rose from the dirt in front of some of the beds, which the traders often referred to as "cabins."

Every male resident of a *tulwa* was assigned a particular *tupa* according to his age and rank. The *miko* occupied the west bed or *mikulgi intupa* in many Creek towns. The warriors usually had a bed, called *tustunukulgi intupa*, as did the elders or *henihulgi*, whose bed was called the *henihulgi intupa*. Youths were housed in the *chepanugulgi intupa* or "boys' bed."

Reconstruction of a typical Creek square ground is difficult because of the degree of variation from town to town, but we know that several important functionaries in addition to the *miko* sat in the chief's bed in all the towns. European explorers, Spanish missionaries, and English and American traders quickly learned when they came among the Creeks that it was essential to master the layout of the town square, including who sat where, if they were to survive.

Among those *tulwa* officials and dignitaries who sat in the chief's bed beside the *miko* might be the *yateka* or chief's interpreter, the *heles haya* or medicine man; the *heniha thluko*, also called the *miko heniha*, who acted as chief advisor to the *miko*, and the *miko apokta*, "twin chief," whose particular concern was the activities in, and the maintenance of, the town square.

Old men of the *miko*'s clan, called *mikagulgi*, usually sat in the chief's bed as well. In many towns, they were minor functionaries who had police powers and were responsible for maintaining order.

A peculiar feature of the chief's bed in most squares was a small rear room in which were keep sacred vessels, medicines, and ceremonial objects. Some anthropologists connect this structure with the rear room found attached to some of the buildings discovered atop platform mounds from the earlier periods.

The *tupa* of the beloved men, located on the south, was usually occupied by the *henihulgi*, town elders chosen from a clan different from that of the chief, and by other elders of the town who had distinguished themselves in long service to the *tulwa*.

In the warriors' bed to the north sat all the distinguished warriors--the *tustunukulgi*--of the town, including the *tustunukee thluko* or "big warrior." Warfare was a social institution among the early Creeks. War was practically the only way for a young man to advance. As a consequence, the *tustunukulgi* exerted a powerful influence over the young men of the town.

The *tustunukee thluko*, who was selected by the *miko* and the council of elders, usually directed all matters dealing with the *tustunukulgi*. Not only was the Big Warrior the war chief in most villages, but in times of war he often became the *de facto miko* of the town. The power of the *tustunukee thluko*, which had been tightly restricted to matters of war in the old days, increased after European contact when warfare became almost constant.

Other dignitaries in the warriors' bed might include the *imathla thlukulgi* or "big imathlas," who were the second-ranking war officials behind the *tustunukulgi*, and the *hothlthleebonaya* or "war speaker." Oratory was an art among the Creeks, and a great *hothlthleebonaya*, by swaying public opinion, could exert tremendous influence over his town and the entire nation.

A-cee

A social custom of the Creeks closely identified with their square grounds was the consumption of *a-cee* (sometimes written *asi*), a drink made from the so-called Yaupon holly (*Ilex vomitoria Ait.*), a common ornamental evergreen shrub found in many gardens in the Valley. This is the small holly with the red berries that some locals call the Christmas Berry Tree.

A-cee, the beloved tree, was the source of a tea that was one of their most important medicines. *A-cee* was consumed daily in the town square by males of high standing as a stimulant and purifier. It was also drunk on important ceremonial occasions to evoke the blessing of *Hisagita immisee*, the Supreme Being, and particularly of *Yahola*, a male sky deity associated with purity and with concern for the sick and weary.

A-cee was known to white traders as cassina or the "black drink" because the Indians first parched and then boiled the leaves to make a strong black tea. The Creeks called it "white drink" because they associated it with purification, understanding, brotherhood, and peace. By whatever name, *a-cee* was central to the social and religious life of the Creeks, functioning as their coffee and their consecratory wine.

Although the Yuchi did not take the black drink, many other Indians did. We have documentation of the black drink being consumed by Southeastern Indians from the 16th through the 18th centuries. Archaeologists trace its use back to at least the Mississippian Period, and some think it may have been used by Archaic cultures in America from 5000 B.C. forward.

The Indians did not drink *a-cee* merely because they liked its taste, any more than we drink coffee because we like its taste. *Ilex vomitoria* contains caffeine, a cortical stimulant that excites the central nervous system, especially the cerebral cortex, producing a clearer and more rapid flow of thought and faster reaction time. It also helps relieve or ward off fatigue.

As the species name--*vomitoria*--implies, the Indians sometimes used *a-cee* as an emetic, although the leaves have no emetic properties as such. However, the berries are said to possess emetic properties and may have been used for this purpose. They also appear to have used it as a diuretic, to produce sweating and to ward off kidney stones.

Even when drunk daily, however, *a-cee* was treated with great respect and its consumption was highly ritualized. To the Creeks, *a-cee* was a mind- and spirit-altering substance, one of the most powerful medicines they possessed. The collection of the leaves to make the tea and its preparation were carefully supervised by the *henihulgi*, the elder "second men" who advised the *mikulgi* and supervised public works in the Creek towns. The native habitat of *Ilex vomitoria* is the Atlantic coast from Virginia to central Florida and the Gulf coast west to Texas. It also grows inland as far north as Oklahoma and is found in scattered clumps throughout the Southeastern United States. However, there appears to have been no significant concentrations of the plant in the Chattahoochee River Valley north of the Florida Panhandle. As a result, some anthropologists have concluded that the Creeks of this area traded for *Ilex vomitoria* or transplanted the plant and grew it along with their corn, beans, and squashes.

The Creeks were particularly fond of the tender young leaves that appear on the plant in mid-to late summer, shortly before they held the *Poskeeta* or Green Corn Ceremony, the annual celebration of forgiveness and renewal in which the *a-cee* played an important role.

Preparation

After the leaves of the *a-cee* were gathered, they were toasted in a clay pot. When the leaves were thoroughly browned, water was poured into the pot and the concoction brought to a rolling boil. It was then strained through a split-cane sieve into another earthen jar. The mixture was then either beaten lightly with a whisk or poured from pot to pot to produce a white froth similar to the foam on beer.

The normal containers from which the drink was consumed were either gourds or conch shells. It was usually drunk hot or warm and was almost inevitably accompanied by tobacco, which the Indians smoked daily and also used to evoke a spirit of cooperation and communication between individuals and groups.

Never consumed casually, *a-cee* was always served in a ritualistic fashion, either by elders or youth especially appointed for the task. It was drunk only by males, apparently of high social standing, and the formal manner of its consumption may have aided male bonding. It definitely verified the male pecking

Drinking a-cee.

order in the towns, since the *miko* was served first, followed by the *heniha thluko* or the *tustunukee thluko* and the other officials of the *tulwa* in descending order of rank.

While each man drank deeply from the cup, the official who served the *a-cee* sang out "Yaa-hoo-laa" in a long musical note. The drinker was expected to continue to imbibe the drink until the singer stopped; then the cup was passed and the procedure repeated until all who were entitled to drink had done so.

The Creeks had a war name, *A-cee Yahola*, usually translated "Black Drink Singer," which may have been the title by which the server and singer of the *a-cee* was known. The English rendering of the name of the famous Seminole chief, Osceola, is a corruption of *A-cee Yahola*.

Sometimes huge quantities of *a-cee*--several quarts per man-- were consumed. Afterward, the Indians might force themselves to vomit, spewing the regurgitated *a-cee* six or seven feet. Then, if still inclined, they resumed drinking. It was this practice that gave the plant its scientific name.

White traders who witnessed the regurgitation were astonished and, in some instances, repulsed. It is not clear whether the Creeks actually found the *a-cee* an emetic or whether they were vomiting through learned social response. The effect on the body of large quantities of *Ilex vomitoria* is approximately that of large quantities of coffee. Perhaps the Indians added another ingredient, the berries or salt, which observers failed to notice, when they wanted to vomit.

In any event, the purpose of the regurgitation appears to have been twofold: to physically purge the body of impurities and to symbolically purge the spirit. Afterward, the Indians could listen to talks in the square ground with a clear head and, supposedly, deliberate without prejudice.

As might be expected, the black drink was picked up and used by early European explorers and settlers in the Southeast. The Spanish, in particular, became fond of the drink and addicted to its caffeine content. It was rather widely used as a coffee and tea substitute in the Southeast throughout the colonial and frontier period and again during the Civil War. To this day it is drunk in remote areas of the South, particularly along the North Carolina coast.

Among the names by which *a-cee* is or has been known among white Americans and Europeans are American tea plant, South Sea tea (by which it is known in England), casino-berry tree, coon berry, evergreen cassine, the aforementioned Christmas Berry Tree, and a variety of spellings of yaupon.

Ilex vomitoria is commonly mistaken for dahoon holly, which is a different species altogether.

Two old people, an old woman and her husband, and the nephew of the latter, were living together. One evening the boy went visiting and the old people were alone in the house. When it was dark the boy came back. The door of the house was shut and he heard them talking inside. He went to a corner and stood listening to them. While he stood there one of them said, "Let's go round." "All right," the other answered.

After they had gone out, the boy went in, turned down the bedclothes, and got into bed. He lay there waiting for those old people. One made a noise like a horned owl, and he heard the other sound like that also. While he was still lying there they left the house, but presently he again heard the sound coming back. After going round and round the house they came in. While they were getting the bed ready to lie down in, the old woman turned over the bedding and found the boy lying there.

"Did you hear us go out?" she said. "Were you there while we were around?"

"I heard," he said.

"Well, do not tell anyone about us. If you do not tell anyone about us, when we are both dead all the things in this house shall be yours."

"I will not tell," he answered, and all went to sleep.

Next day a little girl who lived near fell sick and died. The old woman heard people crying and started out. When she got to the place, she went to where the little girl was lying dead, dropped upon her body, and wept and rolled about upon it. The boy had an arrow. He got to the place and saw her. The old woman saw *him and stopped crying.*

When she started back the little boy came up and spoke to those people. He said, "Last night that old woman bewitched her so that she died." When he said so, they exclaimed, "That old woman has killed her."

They followed her to her house. When she got there the old man was sitting outside sunning himself. She came up and said, "Come in. They want to kill us," and he ran in and shut the door. Then the people surrounded the house and set it on fire and both were burned.

A Hitchiti Tale

XII

The Spiritual System

The Creeks of the Valley were a deeply spiritual people. They acknowledged a supreme being, whom they called *Hisagita immisee*, the "Master of Breath" or "Breath Holder," but their system of belief was quite different from Christianity, Judaism, or Islam. In fact, we are not certain precisely what or who *Hisagita immisee* represented in the Indian pantheon. Some Creeks said the old term for

Valley Indians revered the sun or hasee. their supreme deity was *Ibofunga*, "the one above us," or *Puyafekcha thluko*, "the great spirit." The latter term, however, may be a creation of Christian missionaries. Beyond this, they would say little. The Indians of the Valley were notoriously reluctant to speak of their spiritual beliefs and never really understood the inclination of Europeans and Americans to do so.

It does appear likely, however, that at the time of first white contact, *Hisagita immisee* was not an anthropomorphic god and may have been directly associated with the sun. *Hisagita immisee* also appears to have been associated with fire, which was a central element in Creek religious ceremonies and rituals. All Creeks and other Valley Indians professed the most profound reverence for fire, the sun's representative on earth. We know from our study of the prehistoric period in the Valley that sun worship and veneration of fire goes back at to least Woodland

160

times and probably much further. During the Mississippian Period, clear evidence of sun worship can be found in the surviving symbols of the Southeastern Ceremonial Complex and in the accounts of the De Soto expedition. The French documented sun worship among the Natchez on the Mississippi River in the late 17th and early 18th centuries. It is found among all the native people of the Southeast. The Yuchi thought the sun was female and the moon male. So, most likely, did the Creeks.

Importance of Nature
Perhaps the greatest difference between Christianity and the beliefs of the Creeks and other Indians in the Southeast had to do with how the Indians related to the natural world. Not only did the early people of the region venerate the sun and moon and other natural, inanimate elements--the wind, for example--but they also saw humankind as no more important than the other elements in creation. In the far more anthropomorphic and paradoxical belief system of the Europeans, humankind was said to be simulataneously created in God's image and doomed to spiritual inadequacy.

Traditional Christianity, for example, teaches the natural depravity of man consequent to the fall or expulsion from the garden of Eden. Nature, in the main, is seen as evil, corrupt, something to rise above, control and exploit. The Indian point of view was precisely the opposite. Nature was divine and humankind was a part of nature. To be in accordance or balance with nature was good--*heethlee*. Evil--*heethleko*, i.e. not good-- was to be out of balance with nature, that is, to set oneself apart from or to be at odds with nature.

This fundamental disagreement set the stage for nearly 400 years of violence and misunderstandings between European settlers and native Americans. Because white men, called *esteehatkee* by the Creeks, thought they had dominion over nature, the Indians viewed then as a profoundly immoral and ignorant people. They thought, in short, that they were savages--

seminoli, "wild men."

They were closer to Christian beliefs, however, in dividing the world into an Upper or Sky World and a Lower or Under World. The Sky World was associated with past or ancient time and with order, discipline, balance, and purity. The Under World was associated with the future, with disorder, change, and, interestingly, creativeness. These concepts gave a profound duality to the Creek belief system, which also included This World, where we all live. The physical earth was viewed variously as a flat plane overarched with a vault, an island floating in a sea, or a square supported by four cords. Native Americans were surprised at the European notion that the earth was round.

Suhka, *oppossum*

Although the native people of the Valley appear to have had no notion of heaven or hell, they did believe men and women had souls which, after death, traveled to the West on the "spirits' road"--*puyafekchulk-nennee*--that is, as we say, the Milky Way, to the darkening land.   Although they built no mounds, they were much preoccupied with the dead, whom they called "the landowners," and much disturbed by the notion of ghosts, spirits, and witches.   Nature was for them still filled with wonder and mystery, and, as a consequence, they were not ashamed to admit fear and awe in its presence.

Our own era, on the other hand, has been characterized by progressive demystification of nature, so much so that it is sometimes difficult for contemporary Americans to understand the spiritual and psychological world of native Americans.

Charles Hudson of the University of Georgia, and other students of the mind of Southeastern Indians, have worked out some generalizations that help us bridge the gap between our world and the world inhabited by earliest people of the Valley:

* Specific environmental conditions, including particularly animals, plants, climate, and geography, shaped the Indians' religious beliefs and, as a result, their society as a whole. This is what is meant when we say the native people of the Chattahoochee River Valley lived locally in a way contemporary residents can scarcely imagine.

* For the Creeks and for all other Southeastern Indians, similarity in appearance equalled similarity in nature. That is, essence is manifested in the visible world. If you eat deer meat, you ingest the essence and characteristics of that animal. As a result, you will be able to run swiftly and escape your enemies. However, if you eat opossum, which many Creek warriors refused to do, you would likely be slow afoot, sluggish, and have weak eyesight.

For a people who possessed neither the microscope nor the telescope, the belief that a thing's appearance reflected its nature or character was natural, but it had far-reaching consequences and influenced virtually all aspects of the Indians' social life, religion, and even medicine.

* As is the case with most "primitive" people, the Creeks tended to invest both animate and inanimate objects with supernatural powers. Animals were animals, but they might also be something else in disguise. Likewise, a rock or crystal could possess magical properties. As a result, the Creeks were a spirit-haunted people, much bedeviled by strange creatures, monsters, ghosts, and witches.

* The Creeks' belief system, and perhaps that of all Southeastern Indians, attempted to reconcile all observable phenomena--animal, mineral, human, or spiritual--in a closed system. It could be argued that Christianity attempts the same, but much of Christianity, at least as we know it in our age, admits scientific discovery, symbolic or metaphorical

interpretation of scripture, and limitations on human knowledge. The Creek system of belief was, by contrast, totally intolerant. To admit one change or disagreement was to challenge the whole system.   An analogy might be fundamentalist Christianity that insists that every word of the Bible is literally true.

This closed system of belief was another aspect of Creek life that had profound consequences and, ultimately, limited the Indians' ability to maintain their own societal stability and respond to the challenge of the white man.

* The Creeks' system of belief emphasized order, interrelatedness, analogy, similarity, separateness, balance, purity, and peace--not justice, as Hudson has observed. Because their system had to explain everything, including the animal and plant orders, Indians had to come up with a system for classifying all visible phenomena. For example, they divided the animal world into three basic categories based on visible physical similarities:

Nokosee, *black bear*

There were four-footed animals that walked on all fours, such as the wolf, raccoon, deer, dog, and the like.

There were birds, feathered creatures that had wings and flew.

And there were vermin--snakes, salamanders, frogs, and the like--which were associated with the Lower World.

Since the world had to be a closed system of neatly interlocking categories, the Creeks were concerned with reconciling such apparent contradictions as the bat--a four-footed animal that had wings and flew; the owl--a bird that saw better at night; the bear--a four-footed animal that sometimes walked on its hind legs; and the like.   They did so, says Hudson, by making these animals special cases or "anomalies."

Strange Creatures

Owls and bats and numerous other animals and even plants had a special place in the spirit world of the Creeks, who were much troubled by apparitions and nightmarish creatures of the netherworld. It is important to realize, however, that these creatures--we would call them ghosts, witches, and monsters-- were essential elements in the Indians' belief system. They were there to explain some otherwise inexplicable phenomenon. The Creek or Muskogulgi world view sought to explain all observable phenomena. It admitted of no coincidences, no unexplained occurrences, no accidents. This meant that there was a cosmological significance--a motive--operating in nature. For example, if a deer hunter returned from a hunt and became ill, it was because he had offended the deer spirit. If a woman miscarried, it was because she was impure. If a warrior mislaid his knife, a spirit took it.

This is not as odd as it may appear at first. Even today we sometimes resort to spirits to explain what we regard as otherwise inexplicable events. When someone does something out of character we might say the "Devil made him do it" or "she was possessed." We say "God moves in mysterious ways" to explain some terrible tragedy. Belief in evil spirits was not then and is not now restricted to native Americans. It is, in fact, widespread throughout the world.

Nevertheless, offending a spirit was serious business to the Indians of the Valley and called for an act of atonement and purification. The Creeks and other Indians spent a good deal of time ritually purifying themselves for such offenses.

No Devil

So far as we know, the Creeks knew of no devil or similar character prior to contact with whites. One early traveler among the Indians of this area does record an *estee facheseko*--"person without integrity"--but this notion appears nowhere else in historical literature and, in fact, referred to certain mythical beings inhabiting the Okefenokee Swamp.

Of spirits and monsters and curious creatures, however, there were plenty. Many of these spirits were identified with specific natural phenomena such as rain, thunder, lightning, wind, or with common animals, including the snake, bear, eagle, buffalo, cougar, and deer. They appear over and over in the folk tales and myths of the Creeks and other Southeastern Indians. Thus the Creeks, as did many early people, animated nature. They believed animals could talk, for example, and that trees, rocks, and plants had spirits, also.

Sabia

Rocks, for example, possessed special properties, especially crystals. The Creeks called such powerful charms *sabia* and believed they were especially effective in hunting. Crystals, or minerals which resembled crystals--or even plants whose flowers resembled crystals--were good medicine in love, as well, and might aid their possessor in war, public speaking and almost any undertaking. Anyone fortunate enough to own a *sabia* treated it with great respect, often partially wrapping it in white buckskin and carrying it in a special pouch along with some red paint. On a hunt, the hunter would put a little of the paint on his face and sing a *sabia* song, the latter a ritual formula intended to have some desirable effect on the game he sought, such as blinding it to his approach or making it deaf to human sounds.

A *sabia* was such powerful medicine that its owner often did not dare keep it on his person or even in his house. It was only handled when its power was needed, and even then the *sabia* songs, which appear to have been of many different types, had to be sung. If the charm were handled carelessly or without proper respect for its power, Valley indians believed its owner would suffer disastrous consequences.

Powerful natural forces, such as thunder and lightning were revered by the natives of the Valley. They also personified these forces by making them into serpents, giant birds and other creatures. The rainbow which the Creeks call *Oskee-entacha*, "cutter-off of the rain," was believed to be a giant snake.

Sky Creatures

Yahola and Hayuya were two important male deities of the Upper or Sky World. They were avuncular figures of extreme purity, benefactors of the sick and weary, and they were frequently evoked in cleansing and purification ceremonies. Yahola was also associated with the ceremony of the a-cee or black drink. Hayuya may have been associated with fire.

Estakwanaya, *Tie-snake*

Thunder Man and Thunder Snake produced thunder and lightning respectively, and there was a Thunderbird who seems to have been set in opposition to a Tie-snake or Horned Water Serpent in the Under World.

As might be expected from a people so exposed to the weather as were the Creeks, the wind was a deity of enormous significance and power. The chief clan of the Creeks in our area was the Wind clan, and there are numerous Creek stories and legends about the power and importance of the wind. There also seems to have been some sort of Celestial or Sky Snake, which lived on dew and leaves and may have been associated with the whirlwind. Hurricanes (*hotulee thluko*, "great wind") bedeviled the Indians of the Valley in their time just as they do us today.

Then there was *Subuktee*, a giant toad who lived in the sky and threatened to swallow the sun or the moon during an eclipse. The only way he could be prevented from doing so was if the Indians could create enough noise to scare him away. Accordingly, during an eclipse of either luminary, Valley Indians would shout and pound their drums or do anything to create a racket. During historic times, they would bang pots and pans and fire off their guns.

Creatures Of The Under World

Water, which all Southeastern Indians regarded with superstitious awe, was of particular importance to the Creeks.

Not only did they bathe ritually in water every morning, but they also associated many strange creatures and spirits--"masters of the waters"--with the creeks, lakes, rivers, and sinkholes of this area. Perhaps water, with its mysterious origins in the earth, was thought of as concealing openings into the Under or Below World, the province of disruptive and sometimes threatening forces in Creek belief. Of course, in the Chattahoochee River Valley, water really was the province of some strange creatures, including snakes, alligators, frogs, beaver, spiders, and garfish. So it is not surprising that the Creeks would have associated spirits and even monsters with water.

Of all these creatures, none constellated as many different spirits and powers as the snake, called *chetto* by the Creeks, an omnipresent and often dangerous fact of daily life. The Creeks appear to have lived in mortal fear of offending the snake spirit-- they were sure to be fatally bitten if they did so--and many Indians called snakes *Pucha*, "Grandfather." There were few if any circumstances under which Creeks would kill a snake deliberately.

One of the most curious and powerful of the water creatures was the Tie-snake or *Estakwanaya*, which lived in deep pools and sometimes captured and drowned swimmers or dragged them down into underwater caverns that were, in effect, miniature villages and towns. On land, the Tie-snake traveled by a series of jumps or flips--many of the Creeks' spirit creatures moved strangely. Although short, the Tie-snake was very strong, strong enough, in fact, to carry a man or a horse on its back. It was most apt to be encountered when a person was alone in the deep

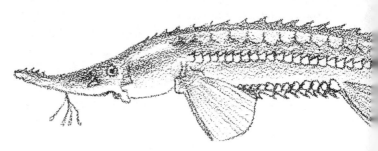

Nokchapee-haukee, *Atlantic sturgeon*

woods. Limestone sinks and springs appear to have been its favorite habitats.

Then there was the great Sharp-Breasted Snake, a real monster that changed its place of residence during a rainstorm and tore up the earth as it moved along. The deep furrows it left in the soil, the trees it split in its passage, and the other signs it left on the earth clearly indicated to the Indians that such a snake existed. Some authorities think the furrows and shattered trees left by the Sharp-Breasted Snake were, in reality, the effects of lightning. If so, the Indians may have conceived the Sharp-Breasted Snake to explain such physical phenomena.

Perhaps the most revered of the snake creatures was the Horned Snake, which lived in water and had horns like a deer. Its horns were a special charm for hunters. Harmless to man, the Horned Snake could lure animals to its den where it killed them and ate only the tips of their noses. To possess merely a fragment of a horn from one of these monsters would greatly aid a hunter in his pursuit of game.

There were various other strange snake-like creatures, most of them identified with water. And there were many other types of water creatures as well, including water tigers, water bear, water calves, and even a long-haired water person about four feet tall.

Creatures of the Forest

The woods and swamps of the Chattahoochee River Valley were haunted places for the Indians who lived here. Even common creatures of the woods--lizards, frogs, birds--could be

possessed of magical properties and might, at any moment, reveal themselves to be supernatural beings in disguise.

One such creature was the small, common tree lizard, which the Creeks called *hachuklepa*. There was a giant version of the *hachuklepa* that lived inside trees and was large enough to eat a man. Sometimes it would emerge from hiding and chase human beings through the woods.

Other denizens of the forests were:

Nokos oma, "like a bear," which was about the size of a black bear but bore enormous tusks. It raced thought the forest with cries of "Kup! Kup! Kup! Kup!"

Wak oma--"like a cow"-- looked like a steer but moved in single file alternately.

Hachko faskee--"sharp ears"--were bushy-tailed creatures who always traveled in pairs and only traveled north-south-- never east or west.

And there were many other animal monsters lurking in the forest. *Estee-papa*--"maneater"--was a supernatural cat-like creature that consumed people.

Not all threatening animals were monsters, however. Any owl, which the Indians associated with death, was likely to be a frightening presence to the Creeks, who also held various superstitious beliefs about eagles, wolves, crows and snakes.

There were also strange, sometimes threatening human-like creatures in the woods. Among these were the "little people" or fairies, who sometimes caused sickness, particularly mental disorders, and giants whose eyes opened vertically rather than horizontally.

The Creeks, to whom such mythical monsters were all too real, spent a good deal of their time worrying about offending the spirits of the sky, water, air, and forest. They had elaborate rituals and common formulas or prayers designed to propitiate the supernatural creatures that inhabited the Valley.

The Knowers

Special individuals called *keethlulgi* or "knowers" among the Creeks were considered to be invested with spiritual powers far beyond the ordinary. Early white traders, searching for an English word that would convey the extraordinary powers the Indians attributed to the *keethlulgi*, settled on "prophets," a not very satisfactory term that stuck.

A *keethla* was not a shaman or medicine man or priest, although he combined the power, knowledge, and wisdom of all three. He was an exceptional individual gifted with deep spiritual and psychological wisdom and a sort of second sight. *Keethlulgi* were rare men, and they were usually consulted in matters of tribal, clan, or individual importance. Finding an adequate counterpart in our society to the *keethla* is difficult, but perhaps the late American mythologist and teacher Joseph Campbell or the psychiatrist Carl Jung come closest.

Keethlulgi could--or so the Creeks believed--diagnose illness, foretell death and crime, interpret dreams, deflect bullets and arrows, bring rain, talk in tongues, and perform many wonderful and magical feats. However, their main function in Creek society seems to have been to help restore order or balance with nature.

As we discussed earlier, the Creek system of belief demanded that people stay pure and in balance with nature. If, by virtue of some thoughtless act, one offended, say, the animal spirits or the spirits of the dead, suffering was sure to follow. It was then that the magical powers of the *keethla* and lesser ritual specialists would be called upon to set things right.

Keethlulgi were not merely somatic physicians. The treating of actual physical diseases was left to priests or doctors called *alektchulgi* or *heles-hayulgi*, "medicine makers." The knowledge of the *keethlulgi* embraced the entire culture of the Indians and was cosmic in scope. During the historic period, the fame of certain Creek *keethlulgi* spread throughout the towns of the Creek Confederacy and, indeed, among other Indian tribes as well.

Estee Poskulgi

The *alektchulgi* and *heles-hayulgi* belonged to a group of learned men called *estee poskulgi*--"fasting men." Women practiced medicine, too, although we do not know to what extent. There definitely were wise or "beloved women" among the Creeks, and as we have discussed earlier, they were often consulted in important tribal matters. However, the great majority of the *heles-hayulgi* were men who had been carefully schooled in the nature of disease and in the healing medicines. The training these individuals received was known as *poskeeta*, "to fast." This is the same name--*Poskeeta*--the Indians gave to their most important annual ritual ceremony, which we know as the busk or Green Corn Ceremony and which also involved fasting.

Heles-hayulgi were important and often powerful figures. They were responsible for purifying and sanctifying tribal medicine, for warding off ghosts, protecting the public health, and conducting important ritual observances, including parts of the annual busk or Green Corn Ceremony. They were also essential functionaries in warfare, and they almost always accompanied a war party to ward off bad luck and assure victory. Some were thought to control the weather, although this was an unpredictable and sometimes dangerous business: in periods of extreme bad weather, weather controllers were often put to death.

John R. Swanton, the principal authority on the early Creeks, recorded some of the methods and initiation rites used in training young men who aspired to become *estee poskulgi*. We might consider such training as a logical extension of the training boys received in the Wilderness School, only in this case it was reserved for only the very best students.

The training sessions were almost always held in the summer

under the direction of a learned man who was himself an *estee poskulgi*, perhaps a *hilis-hayulgi* or even a *keethla*. The Indian agent Benjamin Hawkins, an astute observer of the early Creeks, said the teacher was called *Is-te-puc-cau-chau-thluc-co* or "great leader."

A small band of youths, never exceeding four, would approach such a leader and ask to be trained. If he were agreeable, they would repair to an isolated creek where they would not be interrupted. To further ensure privacy, they piled up shrubs and bushes to conceal themselves.

Each candidate or student dug a plentiful supply of *miko hoyanidja*, the red root of a type of willow (possibly *Salix humilis*) that was one of the most important medicines in the Creek pharmacopoeia. The medicine was pounded and boiled with water in a pot. Then the teacher blew into the brew through a cane, sang over the pot, and left. Swanton says blowing into the medicine was supposed to give it virtue. Four times during the morning of their first day, the students drank great quantities of *miko hoyanidja*, which caused them to vomit. They ate nothing.

At noon, the teacher came back in and gave the young men some elementary instruction. Much of the information was conveyed in songs and formulas which the novices had to memorize on the spot. The teacher went away again to return just before sundown. He gave the boys, who were usually between 15 and 17 years old, according to Hawkins, more instruction. Then he left them alone again.

The first thing the candidates were taught was how to treat flesh, bowel, and head wounds. They were taught how to treat the wounds physically and they also were given the proper songs to sing so that their medicine would be powerful. The songs or formulas had to be repeated exactly as given by the instructor, who would criticize the boys and correct their mistakes.

The students continued to fast and study for four days. They learned to treat many disorders and injuries in addition to wounds. The fasting was supposed to induce dreams which the teacher would interpret.   At the end of the fourth day, the students made a blanket tent and brought hot stones inside. Water was poured over the stones and the boys were thoroughly steamed.   Then they bathed in the creek and went home.

This ended the first session.   Many of the young men went no further in training.   However, after a month or two had passed, those who wished further instruction would gather again at the creek with their teacher.   Another four-day session would be held.   A particularly ambitious and able youth might request further sessions, perhaps as many as four or five.   Then he could ask for an eight-day session, a rigorous experience few completed.   Finally, as a sort of Ph.D., he could ask the teacher for a 12-day session.   If the student completed this final session successfully, the teacher would dig a trench in the ground, ask the student to lie down, place a hollow cane in the student's mouth, and cover him with earth.   Then he would pile leaves over the earth and set them on fire.   When the fire had burned out, the teacher would order the student to get up.

Thus was the novitiate buried to be reborn one of the *estee poskulgi*.   As a sign of his new status, he was entitled to wear a horned owl feather in his headdress.   He might also wear a buzzard's feather, a sign that he could treat gunshot wounds, or a fox's skin because he could cure snake bite.

Walnut-cracker lived at a certain place. He liked walnuts, so he gathered a great number of walnuts and made a pile of them. He also had things with which to crack them. He ate walnuts all day. That was the way he lived, and when he died they buried him at the place where the walnuts were.

Some time afterwards a man out hunting passed near that place and found a great number of walnuts there. He cracked and ate one and, finding it good, came back during the night and got some more walnuts there. He leaned his gun up against a tree, sat down, and cracked walnuts.

While he was sitting there a man came out of a house close by and heard some one at the place where Walnut-cracker had lived. He listened and heard the cracking plainly. Looking closely in that direction he saw a man sitting there looking like the man who had died and been buried. Then he went back into the house and said, "That man who always cracked walnuts and died and whom we buried sits at the same place cracking walnuts."

All went out and looked toweard the place, and sure enough there was some one sitting there. Then they crept toward him.

A lame man who thought a lot of the former Walnut-cracker, and after he had died had been talking a great deal about him, said, "Take me along on your back. I want to see him." One man took him on his back and all started.

When they got near, they thought it was a ghost. They stopped in fear, but the lame man whispered, "Take me a little farther so that I can see him."

His companion took him farther on and stopped.

The Walnut-cracker did not see them. He only kept on cracking walnuts.

Then the lame man said again, "Take me a little farther again so that I can see him." He was taken still closer, and when they got very close the man who was cracking walnuts looked back and, seeing so many people standing about, jumped up quickly, leaped toward the place where his gun stood, seized it, and ran off.

When the people saw him moving about they also ran. The man who had the cripple on his back threw him off and ran home.

The man who was crippled jumped up and ran. That man had nothing the matter with him any longer. He outran the others and reached his house and could walk ever after.

Therefore, if a person has a sudden fright, sickness may disappear.

This is the way they tell it.

A Creek Tale

XIII

Disease and Cure

Medicine bundle

Perhaps nothing so separates us from the world of the Indians of the Chattahoochee River Valley as does the development of modern science, particularly the practice of medicine. The Creeks thought the major causes of human illness were the vengeful spirits of animals, real and mythical. The sun also caused diseases, as did the moon, dead bodies, ghosts, thunder, fire, and the rainbow.

These beliefs are not so strange as they might appear when we recall the Creeks' insistence on staying in balance with nature. They were much preoccupied with maintaining this balance and with avoiding offense to the animals upon which they depended for sustenance. Indian hunters almost always asked forgiveness, in the form of a ritual prayer, from the animals they killed. Usually, they sacrificed part of the animal by dropping a portion of its flesh in a fire. On the big winter hunt, the entire carcass of the first deer killed might be so sacrificed.

Nevertheless, despite their best efforts, the Creeks believed the animals they hunted and ate were inevitably offended in some

178

manner, usually when a hunter forgot to ask forgiveness or when he unwittingly offended his prey.

As might be expected, deer were thought by the Creeks to be one of the main causes of disease. Usually, a specific disease or complex of diseases was associated with a particular animal. Often the illness reflected some characteristic of the animal with which it was associated, as when diseases of the lung that produce phlegm were associated with fish and snails. The eye of the deer was supposed to produce diseases of the eye in man; the deer's tongue was associated with human diseases of the tongue, and so on.

Although precise scientific identification of the diseases associated with particular animals by the Creeks is extremely difficult, some of those suggested by researchers are:

Deer disease: rheumatism, swelling and severe pains in the joints.

Bear disease: infections producing high fevers.

Rabbit disease: possibly kidney infection. Pain in lower abdomen, difficulty in urination, passing blood.

Raccoon disease: possibly dietary disease in children. Patient has distended stomach and is generally in poor health.

Squirrel disease: gum inflammation.

Dog disease: possibly food poisoning. Severe pains in the stomach and bowels accompanied by vomiting.

Panther disease: cholera.

Opossum disease: croup in children.

Eagle disease: crick in the neck.

Despite this rather impressive list of ailments, the 18th-century traveler William Bartram found the Indians of the Valley healthier than the whites he encountered. So far as is known, heart disease and cancer were relatively unknown among the Indians of the Valley. Smallpox, of course, was unknown until introduced by Europeans, after which it caused great suffering and death.

Perhaps the disease most feared by the Valley Indians was rheumatism or deer disease. Prior to the introduction of horses by the Spaniards in the 16th century, the only mode of land travel for Southeastern Indians was their own feet. A person with rheumatism was frequently unable to hunt or draw a bow and was incapable of running to escape enemies.

Plant Cures

The principal treatments for all diseases came from medicines provided by the vegetable kingdom, which the Creeks thought had been created specifically to mediate between mankind and the animal kingdom. Plants were not only friendly, but they also provided cures for specific diseases. As a consequence, the Creeks had an extensive knowledge of herbal medicine and a pharmacopoeia of several hundred plant derivatives.

Four of the greatest medicines of the Creeks were *a-cee, miko hoyanidja, pasa,* and *heles hatkee.* Either separately or in combination, these plant medicines were used to cure a variety of illnesses and to mark ceremonial occasions of the highest importance. Thus the same medicine might have both a secular and a sacred application.

A-cee (Ilex vomitoria), the Creek tea or coffee, was consumed daily by men in both a social and a spiritual context. As we have seen, it functioned primarily as a stimulant and as a purgative. It does not seem to have been used very often in the treatment of specific illnesses. We cannot, however, be sure of this. The consumption of *a-cee* by Indians of the Southeast is thought to be an ancient practice, perhaps stretching back into pre-Woodland times. Minute amounts of stimulants would have had a profound effect on people not accustomed to them, and it may be that *a-cee* was more important in the treatment of illness than we think.

Miko hoyanidja (Salix spp.), "passer by of the chiefs" or "chief's purgative," was made from the pounded roots of a species of willow or Salix. Commonly called red root, *miko hoyanidja* was an especially important and powerful medicine among the Creeks, who boiled the root pulp in water. The resultant concoction, which was drunk hot or cold, was considered effective in the treatment of fevers, malaria, biliousness, dropsy, and rheumatism. *Miko hoyanidja* was one of the most effective of Indian medicines. It contains salicylic acid, which is related to our aspirin. It was also one of the great medicines of the *Poskeeta* or Green Corn Ceremony.

Pasa (Erynigium yuccaefolium), the button snake root of whites, was used to treat neuralgia, kidney troubles, diseases of the spleen, and snake bite. It was prepared in the same manner as *miko hoyanidja*. *Pasa* was the second great medicine of the *Poskeeta,* where it was consumed in large quantities along with *miko hoyanidja*. Those who drank it said that it had a soothing effect well calculated to induce a state of tranquility and receptiveness. This is a curious note because *pasa* was also the Creeks great "war physic," and they never failed to drink it before taking to the warpath. It may have been taken as a purgative or ritual cleansing agent.

Heles hatkee, "white medicine," is known to us as ginseng. A tea made from pounded roots of the plant was widely used by the Indians of the Southeast, including those in the Chattahoochee River Valley, to treat shortness of breath, croup in children, as a coagulant, and to keep away ghosts. It was also taken as a general health tonic and was mixed with a variety of other medicines to make up compound curatives.

Other important Creek medicines:

Notosa, angelica *(Angelica atropurpurea)*, was chewed to relieve back pains and stomach disorders. Sometimes it was dried, mixed with tobacco, and smoked.

Wilana, wormseed *(Chenopodium ambrosioides)*, was made into a tea and used as a spring tonic. It was also used to purify the square ground during the *Poskeeta*. Today, many people know this plant as Mexican Tea.

Acheena, cedar, was taken both internally and externally, either as a spring tonic or, when pounded into a poultice, to relieve aches and pains.

Kupapaska, spicewood *(Benzoin aestivale)*, was sometimes

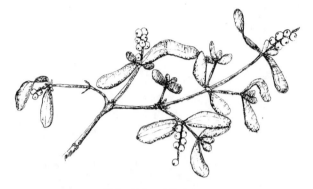

Toh-elleko, *Mistletoe*

Kofochka-thluko, *Horsemint*

Heles-hatkee, *Ginseng*

Pasa, *Button Snakeroot*

Weso, *Sassafras*

Acheena, *Cedar*

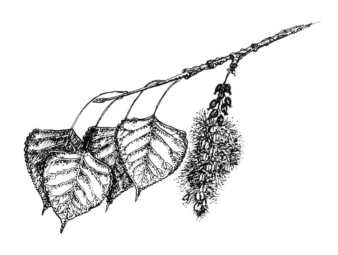

Tathlta-hka, *Cottonwood*

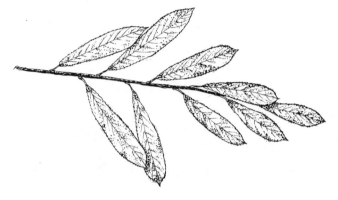

Miko Hoyanidja, *Dwarf Gray Willow ?*

Hechee-atchulee pakpakee, *Tobacco*

A-cee, *Yaupon holly*

drunk simply as tea. Patients suffering from vague aches and pains were sometimes steamed in a bath of spicewood. Taken in combination with *miko hoyanidja*, it was said to induce vomiting.

Kofochka-thluko, horsemint or a bergamot *(Monarda spp.)*, was used as protection against ghosts, to ward off rheumatism, and to induce perspiration. Apparently, this medicine was associated with death, or at least with mortuary practices. When someone died, family members bathed in it as protection against the ghost of the deceased.

Katohwa, honey locust *(Gleditsia triacanthos)*, was chopped and added to water to make a bath to ward off disease, particularly smallpox.

Ala, buckeye *(Aesculus hippocastanum)*, was used to treat consumption. This is the same plant the Indians of the Valley used to poison or stupify fish. It contains a dangerous glycoside and had to be treated with great respect. The devil's shoestring *(Tephrosia spp.)*, called by the Creeks *aloneskee*, was used in the same manner, plus it was believed to be effective in treating impotence.

Adokthlu lastee, so-called black weed or wild indigo *(Baptisia tinctoria)*, was used as a soothing bath for children, who were sometimes given a weak infusion to drink. This is a dangerous plant that has been known to poison cattle.

Chetto yekcha heleswa, "medicine of the strong snake." This is sarsaparilla *(Aralia spp.)* of some kind. An infusion was made from the pounded roots to treat urinary problems and for pleurisy.

Toh-elleko, mistletoe *(Phoradendron flavescens)*, was used sparingly and in combination with other medicines to treat lung ailments. This is another dangerous plant which has been known to poison human beings. The Indians of northern California used mistletoe as an abortifacient and to prevent pregnancy. The Creeks may have used it the same way.

Ak-hatka, the sycamore tree *(Platanus occidentalis)*, was used in the treatment of tuberculosis. So were white birch, yellow pine, and black gum. *Ak-hatka* is one of the more descriptive Creek words. It means "there is light or white down in," a reference to the sycamore's mottled bark.

Tawa chatee, red sumac *(Rhus glabra)*, was a much-used plant by Valley Indians. An infusion was made by boiling its roots to treat dysentery. A tea was made from its colorful spikes, and dried leaves of red sumac were mixed with Indian tobacco and smoked, apparently in the belief that it helped chest ailments.

Kee, the red mulberry *(Morus rubra)*, was important not only as a fruit tree, but also its roots were used to make up an emetic. Some authorities say mulberries, when green, have hallucinogenic properties, but the author knows of no scientific basis for this assertion.

Choska, the post oak *(Quercus stellata)*, provided bark for a drink to treat dysentery.

Eacho impukanu, crabapple *(Malus spp.)*, was used to treat hydrophobia, a much-dreaded disease among Indians of the Valley. The Creek means "deer apple."

Tathlta-hka, the cottonwood tree *(Populus deltoidees)*, was thought by Swanton to be the so-called "warrior tree," various parts of which were used to help patients with broken bones. Splints were made from the inner bark and a decoction was poured over the broken bone to help it set.

Kacho-thluko, the large greenbrier *(Smilax bona-nox*, most likely) was the *kuntee* of the Creeks. They boiled the roots and poured the resulting liquid over ulcers.

Valley Indians probably used prickly ash, sometimes called Hercules-club *(Zanthoxylum clava-herculis)*, to help suppress the pain of toothache. Alabama Indians apparently inserted a bit of root from sweet goldenrod *(Solidago odora)* in a tooth cavity to ease the pain.

It is not known whether the Indians of the Valley possessed anesthetics or effective sedatives. The Natchez chewed Indian tobacco to induce a state of stupefaction, and it may be that local Indians used jimson weed *(Datura stramonium)* similarly.

Jimson weed, which is highly poisonous, contains hyoscyamine, a powerful depressant of the parasympathetic nervous system. The roots and bark of the wild black cherry tree *(Prunus serotina)* may have been pounded and mixed with water to form a sedative. Almost all parts of this tree will yield hydrocyanic acid when steeped in water.

The drugs or potions listed above are only a sampling of the plants used by the Creeks in the treatment of sickness. Nearly every plant that grew in the Chattahoochee River Valley had some use in the Creek medicine cabinet. Many of these herbal medicines were passed down to white and black people in the Valley and became important ingredients in our regional folk medicine.

Ordinarily, individual Creeks did not treat themselves but called on Indian doctors for help. Creek healers, as discussed in the preceding chapter, were of several kinds and included diagnosticians and specialists who treated only certain ailments. Most Creek doctors underwent extensive training, but there were also many amateurs who dispensed home remedies and a special class of "diviners," the *keethlulgi* previously described. A person with a chronic illness might go to a *keethla* for a diagnosis, and then to an *alektcha* or one of several "fasting men," *estee poskulgi*, for treatment.

However, no Creek doctor thought any medicine, which was almost always a liquid composed of vegetable matter and hot water, possessed curative properties in and of itself. To make it effective, the physician first took a straw or hollow reed and breathed into the mixture, thus infusing it with the power and spirit of the supreme deity, *Hisagita immisee*, the "Master of Breath" or the "Breath Holder." Only then did the medicine acquire power to cure.

In actual treatment, a Creek doctor would administer the medicine to the patient while repeating sacred formulas. An important part of a Creek doctor's training to become a member of the *estee poskulgi* consisted of memorizing these formulas, which, as we have seen, required exact repetition to be effective.

Creek medical practitioners also included specialists who treated psychological problems. In fact, early European travelers say that Southeastern Indian doctors were particularly effective in treating emotional disorders. Then, as now, intuition and a thorough knowledge of the human personality were essential to effective treatment of a variety of illnesses. Particularly effective doctors quickly acquired a reputation among the Creeks. People, including white traders, would travel great distances to be treated by them.

It was out upon the ocean. Some sea-foam formed against a big log floating there. Then a person emerged from the sea-foam and crawled out upon the log. He was seen sitting there. Another person crawled up, on the other side of the log. It was a woman. They were whites. Soon the Indians saw them, and at first thought that they were sea-gulls, and they said among themselves, "Are they not white people?" Then they made a boat and went out to look at the strangers more closely.

Later on the whites were seen in their house-boat. Then they disappeared. In about a year they returned, and there were a great many of them. The Indians talked to them but they could not understand each other. Then the whites left.

But they came back in another year with a great many ships. They approached the Indians and asked if they could come ashore.

They said, "Yes." So the whites landed, but they seemed to be afraid to walk much on the water. They went away again over the sea.

This time they were gone a shorter time; only three months passed and they came again. They had a box with them and asked the Indians for some earth to fill it. It was given to them as they desired. The first time they asked they had a square box, and when that was filled they brought a big shallow box. They filled this one too. Earth was put in them and when they were carried aboard the ship the white men planted seed in them and many things were raised. After they had taken away the shallow box, the whites came back and told the Indians that their land was very strong and fertile. So they asked the Indians to give them a portion of it that they might live on it. The Indians agreed to do it, the whites came to the shore, and they have lived there ever since.

A Yuchi Tale

XIV

Social Customs

Creeks boys and girls born in the Chattahoochee River Valley were treated differently from birth to puberty. Indeed, throughout their lives Indian men and women were usually confined to rigidly determined, separate roles based upon tradition, sex, and the struggle for survival in a hostile environment.

No matter what time of year or what the weather conditions, Creek children--*hopwetakee*, from *hopwewu*, "child"--were born out of doors or in huts some distance from the family living quarters. Women delivered their children alone and remained alone with the child for some time after birth. An older woman or midwife might assist the mother after delivery but usually not during.

In extreme cases, when the mother was ill or in protracted labor, a *heleshaya* or *alektcha* might prepare a special medicine (*heleswa*) of slippery elm and administer it to the woman, calling on the sky-god Yahola for help. This is an example of the Creeks' belief in sympathetic magic, a belief rooted in the assumption that a thing's visible properties were innate and communicable. However, most Creek women bore their children without complaint, amazing early European travelers and white traders with their toughness in childbirth.

Shortly after a child was born, no matter what the weather conditions, it was often taken to the nearest body of water and bathed--even if the mother had to break the ice to do so. There are stories of Creek mothers rolling their children in the snow right after birth to toughen them up. Water might be sprinkled on the child's tongue before the mother began to nurse it.

Male infants were wrapped in cougar skins, girls in the soft hide of a fawn or a buffalo calf. Cougars or panthers were cunning and brave, had excellent eyesight and were formidable hunters. It was hoped that the cougar skin would communicate these properties, by sympathetic magic, to the male infant. The young of deer and buffalo were soft and shy, and they sought protection from the rest of the creatures of the forest, qualities then thought desirable in women in the Creek social system.

Although information on abortions among Creek women of the period is sketchy, Creek women did determine whether the child lived or died for a period of a month after birth. If the mother did not want the child, or if the family was unable to care for it, she had the right to put it to death for one moon. Thereafter, if she killed the child she would herself be killed.

However, Creek parents ordinarily doted on their children, and the mother most likely would welcome the child as evidence of her fertility, an important factor among the Creeks in determining the status of women. She might sing it a cradle song or lullaby, several examples of which survive. One was:

"Notka! Notka! Notku-thlit. Che-thlit ma-kit ayunks . . . Notku-thlit. Ma-kit locha ho-pokun. Notcheu-thlit."

Freely translated, it appears to mean, "Go to sleep! Go to sleep! It will go to sleep, your father said before he went terrapin hunting. It will go to sleep."

The family into which the child was born was dominated by the mother and her blood relatives, for, as we have said, descent among the Creeks and most other Southeastern Indians was reckoned matrilineally. A child was a member of its mother's clan, not its father's. This also meant that the child belonged to the mother's *tulwa*.

The mother owned the house (*hutee*) where the family lived and all its domestic implements. Living in the house--or houses, since the Creeks ordinarily lived in compounds consisting of two to four houses--would be a number of the mother's blood relatives, plus her husband. A typical household might consist of the parental unit and children, plus a son-in-law or two, and perhaps the woman's brother or mother and father. No relatives of the woman's husband would live there, and often the husband would himself be absent for long periods, visiting with his mother's family or clan.

Women ran the home but did not do much disciplining, at least not by our standards. Discipline was supplied by the woman's brothers. Children usually looked to their oldest uncle or *pawa* for discipline and direction rather than to their father. Fathers were treated with respect and were not discounted in raising the children, but they were often preoccupied with their own duties as uncles to their sisters' children.

Family Titles

The Creeks had a complex system of names for family members both within and without their clan. Uncles called a nephew *hopwewa* and a niece was *hukpatee*. A boy called his older brother *thlaha*, a younger brother, *chusee*. A sister, younger or older, was *wunwa*. A father called his daughter *chustee* and his son *kputchee*. A stepson was *chukputchee hakee*, "like my son." A grandchild, of either sex, was *osuswa*. A man called his wife *hoktulee*, "old woman," and his mother in-law was *hoktulwa*. A girl called her younger sister *chachusee*, the same term a boy used for his younger brother. An older sister was *chathlaha*, the boy's term for an older brother. She called her brother *chethlwa*. A woman called her husband "old man" and her children of both sexes *chuswa*. A stepchild was *chutchuswa hakee*, "like my child."

White traders who married Creek women had their hands full simply learning the proper titles of her relations.

Some Creek mothers placed their newborn children on cradle boards and kept them there for nearly a year. Hollywood has popularized these useful contraptions--cane or hardwood frames wrapped tightly with cloth and sometimes featuring a mobile dangling before the child's eyes--as papooses. They were very common among the Indians of the Southeast.

Girls were ordinarily given a proper name taken from some event or thing associated with their birth. Among the Chickasaw, who had much in common with the Creeks, these names could be quite romantic--"Blossom," "Flower," "Turtledove." However, examples of names for Creek girls during the time they lived in the Valley are rather rare. John R. Swanton collected a Creek girl's or woman's name in Oklahoma in the early 1900's that was said to be very old-- *Tsianina*--its meaning unknown, which may date back to the Creeks in the Valley.

Adult Creek females seem to have been named for some hunting or war exploit associated with either their fathers or with near male relatives, or perhaps their husbands. These names are anything but poetic, as: *Ana-hki*, "Getting very near the enemy by stratagem"; *Lasaho-yi*, "We saw them at a distance chasing the enemy"; *Anutho-yi*, "Two returning wounded"; and so on.

Boys were usually called by their totem animal--*Fuswa*, "Bird" or *Chetto*, "Snake"--or for some youthful exploit or characteristic until they acquired their war or busk names, by which they were known thereafter.

War Names

The acquisition of a war name--*tasekiya*--was a serious matter for a young man among the Creeks. Indeed, Creek boys trained to be warriors and hunters and to be worthy of proud names almost from infancy. A man without a war name had no status in the town in which he lived. Until he acquired such a name, he was required to wait on other males, fetch water when they needed it, keep dogs out of the town square, and perform other such menial and degrading tasks.

A young man acquired a war name by performing well in battle or in a sortie against the enemy. Rare individuals would sometimes be given a war name as the result of great hunting exploits. In the main, however, a youth had to distinguish himself in an engagement with the enemy. Thus young Creek warriors were usually bellicose and quick to foment warfare, inasmuch as this was practically their only avenue to distinction and success.

The Creeks conferred war names on young warriors with about as much pomp and circumstance as they could mount. Sometimes the ceremony took place at the annual busk or *Poskeeta*, held as soon as the sweet corn was full of milk. To be so honored, a youth had to be nominated by his clan or clan council. He was told what his name would be, and on the appointed day he was present in the town square dressed in his finest apparel. Other young men to be given names were also there, as were the town elders, the *miko*, the *henihulgi* or "second men," the adult warriors or *tustunukulgi*, the *estee achulakulgi* or "beloved men." Town elders would make speeches, often long and eloquent, for the Creeks, who had no written syllabary, were renowned orators.

At the conclusion of the speeches, which might recount the heroic exploits of long-dead warriors and urge all of the young men and warriors present to remain pure--that is, in balance with nature--so they too could succeed in battle, a *heniha* stepped forward and called out the first youth's war name. Sometimes two young men came forward at the same time, received a pouch of Indian tobacco, and were formally presented to the *miko*.

The names they were given were compounds usually made up of their totem name or the name of their town, plus a standardized war name. The latter were of four kinds and rankings:

Hadjo, "mad," "crazy," or "furious in battle."

Fekseko, "heartless."

Imathla, meaning uncertain.

Yahola referring to the long cry given during the ceremony of the black drink.

Another compound name found very frequently is formed by adding *tustunukee* to the totem or town name. *Tustunukee* (sometimes written *tustunugee*) means "warrior," and apparently it was sometimes given as a formal title. The same is true of *miko*.

Swanton says the first four names indicate persons of roughly the same rank or standing and were very common.

Because of U.S. Indian census rolls (complied prior to the removal of the Indians to the West) and treaties and letters bearing the Indians' signatures or marks, we have literally thousands of examples of Indian names from the days when the Creeks lived in this area. Some samples:

Abi-ka hadjo, "Abihka Hadjo."
Fus hutchee fekseko, "Bird Creek Fekseko."
Hotulee imathla, "Wind Imathla."
Acee yahola, "Black Drink Yahola," i.e., Osceola.
Ifa hadjo, "Dog Hadjo."
Ispanee fekseko, "Spanish fekseko."
Kapitka fekseko, "Lye-drip fekseko."
Kasi-ta hadjo, "Cusseta Hadjo."
Kawita tustunuke, "Coweta Warrior."
Kunip yahola, "Skunk Yahola."
Nokos fekseko, "Bear Fekseko."
Ochee hadjo, "Hickory Nut Hadjo."
Pen fekseko, "Turkey fekseko."
Tulahusee imathla, "Old Town Imathla."
Tupusola hadjo, "Daddy-long legs Hadjo."
Wotko fekseko, "Raccoon fekseko."

Creek men sometimes earned several names, which appear to have been awarded on the basis of increasing status. Thus a warrior might be known at different times in his life as *Coweta hadjo*, *Coweta imathla*, *Coweta tustunukee* and *Coweta miko*.

Marriage

Theoretically, Creeks married for life but the double standard was not invented by Europeans. Creek women were free to conduct themselves as they pleased prior to marriage. However, they usually married young and were expected to remain faithful to their husband throughout their lives. Some of them did. Creek men ordinarily had only one wife, but they were free to take another, younger bride if they could afford her. Adultery was sometimes severely punished, however, either by beating or by cropping the noses and ears of both parties.

Ordinarily there was not much ceremony in Creek marriages. The suitor sent his sister or mother to make application for him to the female relations of the girl he wished to marry. The girl's family consulted, not always with her, and if they approved, they informed the proper woman in the suitor's clan. Then the suitor sent gifts to the women of the girl's clan. If they accepted them, the match was made and could be consummated immediately. However, the woman was not considered finally bound until the man had built a house for her, helped her get in a crop, and proved that he was proficient in the hunt.

Divorce was a simple matter of either partner renouncing the other. However, the man was then free to marry right away; the woman had to wait until after that year's *Poskeeta*.

Despite the lack of formality in conjugal relations, there is no evidence that Creek marriages were any less permanent or less happy than our own. Many Creek couples lived out all their years together without complaint or scandal.

Death

Creek warriors were proud and tough and showed no fear of death. Creek women were almost equally fearless, and their toughness in childbirth has already been described. Nevertheless, the Indians of the Valley seem to have had a healthy respect for death, particularly the manner in which someone died and the way the body was disposed of after death.

When a Creek man died, for example, his body was buried

beneath the floor of his home, sometimes right beneath the bed on which his widow would sleep.   If he died in battle, it was vitally important that his body be recovered before it could be scalped and otherwise disfigured by the enemy.   Often the people of a town made a great racket when someone died, driving his spirit away from his house and toward the darkening land in the west.   If this was not done, the dead person's spirit might haunt the house and wreak havoc upon the town itself.   To die bravely in battle was considered the most honorable death, and under no circumstances could a warrior show fear of dying. If captured and tortured, he was expected to taunt and ridicule his captors until he was dead.   Prodigious displays of courage and indifference to pain under such circumstances are recorded.

Space and Time

The Creeks' conceptions of time and number were entirely dependent upon natural phenomena.   As far as we know, they possessed no clocks or tools of measurement until these were introduced by Europeans in the 16th and 17th centuries.

They divided the day into three parts according to the position of the sun--sunrise, noon, and sunset--and their daily activities began at sunrise with a ritual plunge into the river or the nearest stream.   The morning bath was followed by breakfast, which was taken between 7 and 10 a.m., after which they might work in the communal fields, join in the discussions at the square ground, or attend to other matters. The main meal was served at around two, after which there might be a ball game.   The Creeks apparently ate little in the evening, perhaps merely taking a sip of *sofkee*, the hominy gruel of which they were so fond.

There was no week in the Indian calendar, there being no sabbath.   Months were marked by the waxing and waning of the moon.   They divided the twelve moons evenly into a winter and a summer series.   The Creek year began in August, right after the great annual *Poskeeta* or Green Corn Festival.

The winter series of moons was:

August, *Hiyo thluko,* "much heat."
September, *Otowoskutichee,* "little chestnut."
October, *Otowoska thluko,* "big chestnut."
November, *Iholee,* "frost."
December, *Thlufo thluko,* "big winter."
January, *Thlufo chusee,* "little winter."
The summer series was:
February, *Hotulee hasee,* "wind."
March, *Tasahtchuchee,* "little spring."
April, *Tasahcee-thluko,* "big spring."
May, *Kee hasee,* "mulberry."
June, *Kacho hasee,* "blackberry."
July, *Hayuchee,* "little warmth" or "little ripening."

Curiously, despite their awareness of months and years, few Creeks knew their ages. As with most other Southeastern Indians, the Creeks were an extremely fatalistic people and believed the length of a person's life was fixed. Common proverbs when someone died were, "The days appointed him are finished"; or "Such a one was weighed on the path and found light." If an Indian wished to mark the days, he used "sleeps." That is, a week consisted of seven sleeps; two weeks, fourteen sleeps and so on.

Long distances were measured in sleeps, moons, or "sights." A sight was as far as one could see, the rough Indian equivalent of our mile. Thus a distance of five miles was five sights away. A destination requiring two months' travel was two moons away.

The Broken Days

Decimals were tabulated on the fingers. Measures of length were parts of the body, as one finger, one hand. Stick bundles were sometimes used to count the passage of days before important occasions, such as before the annual *Poskeeta* or prior to a national council of war. Each town's *miko* would receive a bundle of such sticks, called "the broken days" by the Creeks, and would remove one stick for each day until only one remained. The last stick indicated the appointed day.

Notched sticks and strings with knots tied in them were also used for counting and as mnemonic devices. So were colored strings of beads and pictographs, although only a few of the latter have survived. Tribal historians used such devices to prompt their memories and recollect important events.

Certain colors were associated with the cardinal points. Red and yellow were the colors of the north, black was associated with the west, blue with the south, and white with the east. Rivers and creeks were sometimes named with colors--as Yellow Creek, Black Creek--indicating direction rather than water condition or color. It may be that the colors assigned to the cardinal directions had emotional content now lost and were part of an ancient spiritual spatial orientation, as seen in the careful

The "Broken Days"

alignment of the platform and burial mounds during prehistoric times and in the square ground of the historic Indians. Anthropologists call such a system "quadripartite."

Seven persons went apart, fasted, and took medicine for four days in order to prophesy. Then they came in and reported to the people what they had found out. Then the people said, "We will select seven persons and find out more."

So they sent out seven persons who fasted and took medicine for seven days. At the end of this time they wondered if they should continue their fast for seven months. They fasted and took medicine until the seven months were completed. Then they asked one another if they could not observe their regulations for a whole year. They accomplished it, but when the time was completed they had become wild and feared to go near the rest of the people, so they went into the woods and stayed there.

They asked one another what they should do and finally said, "Let us turn ourselves into pine trees." At that time there were no iron axes but tools made of flint with which little wood could be cut. But when the white men came and they saw them cutting down pine trees with their axes they said to one another, "That has cut us down."

When the whites went on destroying pine trees they said, "Let us turn oursleves into rock. A rock lies undisturbed on top of the ground." But after they had turned themselves into rocks they saw the white people turn to the rocks and begin to use them in various ways.

Then they made up their minds to go above, saying, "We cannot escape in any other manner." So they rose and went up into the air, where they became a constellation (probably the Pleiades).

A Natchez Tale

XV

Ball Play and Poskeeta

The two greatest social institutions possessed by the Indians of the Chattahoochee River Valley in days past were the ball play, *Pokkecheta*, and the *Poskeeta*. They are probably also the oldest continuously operating social institutions native to the Valley, older by thousands of years than comparable institutions established here since the forced removal of the Valley's native inhabitants to the West in the 1830s and 1840s.

While one could be viewed purely as an athletic contest and the other a religious ceremony, they actually have much in common and are much more substantive than either of

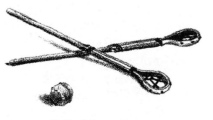

Ball sticks and ball

those definitions admit. Both are rooted deep in the Indians' past and served to link the native people of the Valley with their ancestors who had lived in the same spot hundreds, if not thousands, of years earlier. It is a matter of archaeological record that there are ball yards in Mississippian sites, and certain remains and artifacts--ash-covered hearths, new sand mantles on mounds, cracked or "killed" pottery--suggest that the *Poskeeta* was known to Valley Indians in ancient times. Together, the ball play and the *Poskeeta* involve many of the customs and traditions the native people of the Southeast meant when they spoke of "the old beloved path."

Ball Play

The historic Indians of the Valley were fond of sports,

gambling, and games of all sort. They wrestled, held foot races, played chunkee and a game called "roll the bullet," pitched cane sticks similar to the way we throw dice, and even had a board game something like Pachisi. However, their favorite pastime was *pokkecheta*, a sport for which they had a passion rivaling the contemporary Southern madness for football.

Creek ball play resembled modern lacrosse, which is derived from it, except that the Creeks played with two sticks instead of one--and it was far rougher than the modern game. The Creeks called it "brother to war," and with reason. Participants, who numbered from 50-100 a side, were often injured, sometimes seriously, and deaths were not uncommon.

The Creeks attached tremendous importance to the game, which carried ritual overtones far beyond anything known in our modern-day athletics. It is believed the ball play had a deep mythological history and was at one time a highly ritualized contest involving human sacrifice. Although the Indians of the Valley played the sport with gusto, it was still a serious affair. Some anthropologists say that one of the reasons the Creeks divided themselves into *Hathagulgi* ("white people") and *Chelokogulgi* ("people of a different speech") was to have sides for practice ball games within towns.

Almost every town or *tulwa* had a team, and all of the townspeople took tremendous pride in their athletes. Men and women often wagered heavily on the outcome of the games. A common sight on the sidelines during a game was a pyramid of personal belongings wagered on the outcome. And there are stories of Indians walking home naked after having lost everything--clothes, jewelry, weapons, and horse.

The object of the game was to get a deer-hide ball or *pokko*, about half the size of a baseball, between two upright poles--the goal--set about 10 feet apart. This was worth one point. Goals were located at either end of a more or less level field ranging in size from 150 to 300 yards. Practically the only rule was that the players could not touch the ball with their hands. It had to be passed from man to man with the sticks, called *tokonhee*, which were usually fashioned from hickory and provided with a pocket made of rawhide thongs.

The Indians became very skilled in the use of ball sticks, but passing the ball during a game was no easy feat. The opposition was free to stop another player from passing the ball by any method, including tackling, lashing with the ball sticks, punching, or whatever. No protective padding was allowed--the players wore nothing but moccasins and breechcloths and maybe a panther's or buffalo's tail behind. Members of "white" teams wore a white crane's feather in their hair; "red" players wore an eagle feather. Sometimes the players would paint their bodies in fantastic ways so as to resemble a snake, a bird of prey, or some other powerful and fearsome creature.

Indian ball play was not an activity for the faint of heart. No matter what happened, a participant was not supposed to show anger, which was considered unmanly. All injuries--even death-- during the *pokkecheta* were forgiven, and no one could be the object of clan revenge as the result of having inflicted injury on another during ball play.

The Creeks loved the sport. All males of warrior age were expected to play. The athletes, then as now, were much made over and widely admired. Great ball players were known throughout the Creek nation. Ball players trained at the sport, held regular practices, and played practice games among themselves to keep sharp. There is no evidence that teams had coaches, but the *Tustunukee thluko* or head warrior of the town took a special interest in the team and its members. The sport was definitely associated with manhood and preparation for war. An opponent was called *anthlapa-ya*, "my enemy or opponent."

Ordinarily, real games were played between towns of different fires, that is, between white towns and red towns, as previously described. The games came about when one town challenged another through a rigidly formal process involving the highest-ranking officials, who would meet and have long discussions prior to committing their town to a game. It might take weeks for the representatives of two towns to decide all the issues--how many men to a side, who was eligible, where the game was to be played, how many points would be involved, who the referees would be, and so on. These negotiations were taken very seriously, and those conducting the talks approached in subtlety and deception the general managers and team owners in modern-day athletics. For example, the spokesmen for one town might know that the opposing side had a great ball player who was married but had no children. Thus they would try to have the game played only between men with children. Sometimes only unmarried men could play, and so on.

Preparations to Play

Once the details were worked out and the contract agreed upon, preparations for the contest began. Trees and underbrush were cleared from the site selected for the games. Both sides chose a ball play conjurer, *pokkee-chulkee-alektcha*, or medicine man to make medicine for their team and to cast spells on the opposition. Ball game dances were held the night before the contest. Women and men of the towns took part in the dancing, which was accompanied by drums and the shaking of terrapin rattles. At some point in the evening, the ball players rushed out into the square ground and whooped and hollered, waving their ball sticks in the air and uttering terrible shrieks, a process the Indians called *ya-hkita*.

After the women had gone to bed, the players sat up until morning. It was considered a disgrace to fall asleep until the game had been played. They ate nothing, fasting being a part of the pre-game ritual. Sometimes a "scratcher" would take the jaw of an alligator gar fish or a piece of sharpened bone and scratch each player on the legs and arms. The Creeks believed this strengthened the men and made them run faster.

At the ball field, the players for both sides separated into three position squads--goal, intermediate, and center--and lined up across from each other in the center of the field. Each man threw down his sticks opposite an opponent so that the referees or umpires, called *mudjokulgi*, could count and see that the teams were evenly matched.

Frequently the players would exchange insults or jests while lined up facing each other, and it was at this point that the betting by the fans took place. Then, at a signal from the head referee, the ball was taken to the center of the field, called the *wuskeeta*, and the teams faced off in a scrum.

A gifted orator was usually selected to put the ball into play. True to his calling, he never failed to make a speech for the benefit of the players and spectators, cautioning each side against cheating or fighting and urging the players to do themselves honor by putting forth their best effort. Then he threw the ball up into the air like a jump ball in basketball and announced, "Here goes up a ball for 20 stakes" or some such.

A general melee followed until a player gained control of the ball, broke free from the pack, and hurled the ball toward his goal.

Scoring occurred when a team succeeded in throwing the ball between their goal posts, one goal being counted a point. The game was over when a team reached an agreed-upon total, usually 20 points. Score was kept on the sidelines by planting a stick in the ground for each goal up to ten, then pulling one stick out for each goal from ten to 20.

When his team reached the winning number, the team scorer shouted out "*Elutito toto!*": "He is dead! dead! dead!"

Losing was a catastrophe, not only because of the huge wagers that accompanied the games, but because a town that lost three games in a row had to change sides, from white to red or vice versa, or suffer some other indignity calculated to humiliate and embarrass.

The victors often behaved as bad winners do, crowing over their exploits and demeaning their opponent's manhood. The losers quickly shrank away to nurse their wounds and injured pride and plan their revenge.

Early American settlers in the Valley who witnessed Indian ball games, such as the one played in honor of the passage of the Marquis de LaFayette through Fort Mitchell in 1825, describe them as among the most exciting spectacles they ever witnessed.

The *Poskeeta*

The annual *Poskeeta* or "Fast" of the Creeks, known to whites as the Busk or Green Corn Ceremony, was the most important religious and civic ceremony observed by the Indians of the Chattahoochee River Valley. It was a comprehensive, week-long rite of thanksgiving, forgiveness, and spiritual renewal, a sort of Thanksgiving, Christmas, New Year's Day, and Mardi Gras rolled into one.

Although the *Poskeeta* was specifically timed to coincide with the ripening of the corn in late summer, the fundamental function of the ceremony was purification, both physical and spiritual. All crimes except murder committed during the previous year were forgiven, all quarrels settled. Old fires were extinguished and new ones lit. Old cooking pots and household vessels were broken and replaced with new ones. The square ground and all private and public buildings were cleaned and refurbished, and the people, especially the men, underwent ritual purification through fasting and consumption of herbal medicines.

It was, in the manner in which the Creeks used the word, a "white" celebration, emphasizing peace, harmony, and forgiveness. In many towns, the square ground was entirely covered with clean white sand and the ceremonies were conducted by "priests" dressed in white moccasins, white deer skins, and the feathers of white herons or cranes.

In the old days, the Creeks believed that should they fail to observe the *Poskeeta*, they would suffer terribly, perhaps even perish as a people or society. *Hisagita immisee*, the Master of Breath, had given them the *Poskeeta* and the medicines that accompanied it to protect their health and well-being. Therefore, the old men, the *henihulgi* especially, and priests of the towns were particularly insistent that the ceremony be strictly observed. Anyone who failed to take part was severely punished, fined, or even banished.

In addition to its purifying or spiritual function, the *Poskeeta* brought all the people together at an annual gathering, which helped emphasize custom and tradition and promoted political unity.   There was much speech-making on the part of village elders, who instructed the men to follow the old beloved path of tradition and custom and to be brave in war and productive in the hunt, and who admonished the women to tend to their domestic duties, to be loyal to their husbands and vigilant of their children.

But despite these more mundane functions, the *Poskeeta* was a profound spiritual experience for the Indians of the Valley, one that touched the very soul of the culture, and they were much affected by its solemnity, reverential air, and pomp.

As might be expected among a people so concerned with maintaining a balance with nature, there was a propitiatory or mediating aspect to the ceremony, also.   Animal spirits, including those of game animals and animals considered unfriendly to man (the screech owl, for example) were placated through dances in their honor.

Dances

There were many other dances as well, for the Creeks were a people who enjoyed dancing almost as much as they did ball games.   In addition to the animal dances, the men and women performed the stomp dance, the old dance, the war dance, the

Poskeeta *fire*

feather or peace dance, the drunken dance, and many others. Such dances celebrated the Creek's cultural roots and are evidence of the social and festive aspects of the *Poskeeta* and other festivals.

The time of the Green Corn Ceremony varied from town to town in accordance with the ripening of the corn, which could be anywhere from mid-July to early September. Among the Indians of the Chattahoochee River Valley, it usually took place in late July or early August, the latter the moon of *Hiyo thluko* that began the Creek new year.

As soon as the new corn appeared to be full of milk, the *miko* of a dominant town--Cusseta or Coweta in this area--sent a messenger, called a *ta pala*, to deliver the "broken days" to all the *mikulgi* of lesser towns whose people were expected to attend the big town's *Poskeeta*. Each *miko* removed one stick from the bundle of broken days until only one remained. On that day, the ceremony began in the square ground of the principal town. People of one fire often traveled many miles to be present for the occasion, either staying with clan members or camping out in the woods around the town.

The length of the *Poskeeta* varied considerably from town to town, as did the precise sequence of events. Some *Poskeetas* lasted only four days, some a week, and a few went for eight days. In Cusseta, it lasted eight days, according to the Indian agent Benjamin Hawkins. The Chiaha *Poskeeta* went five days. In Coweta, it lasted five to seven days.

Here is a synopsis of the Cusseta *Poskeeta*:

On the first day, the *tustunukulgi* or warriors cleaned the square ground thoroughly and sprinkled it with fresh white sand. The men drank *a-cee* or the white drink and *pasa*, a decoction of button snakeroot. Four new logs were brought into the square and laid end to end in the shape of a cross. A new fire was kindled in the center of these logs by friction. The women danced the turkey dance. Later men and women took part in the tadpole dance. At night, the men danced the *Heniha opanka*, the dance of the people second in command.

On the second day, the women performed the *Etsa opanka*, or gun dance, and then prepared and served a feast of the new corn.

On the third day, the men sat in the square, probably fasting and taking medicine. They also did this on the sixth and seventh days.

On the fourth day, the women cleaned out their hearths and got new fire from the square. Fasters were allowed to eat salt. That night, the *Opanka chapko* or long dance was held.

On the fifth day, four new logs were brought into the square to replace those burned out. The men drank *a-cee*.

On the eighth and last day, the men drank a mixture of 14 plants, including *miko hoyanidja*. The men covered themselves with ashes and smoked *hechee atchulee pakpakee*, "blossom of the old people's tobacco," believed to have been *Nicotiana rustica*. Everyone bathed in the river. That night, the *Opanka hadjo* or mad dance ended the ceremony.

This sparse recitation hardly touches on the spirit of the ceremony, which ranged from reverential to festive. The *Poskeeta* was of extreme importance to the Creeks. It is worth noting that long after their removal to the West, the Creeks continued to practice the *Poskeeta*, just as they continued their ball play. In fact, both the *Poskeeta* and the *Pokkecheta* remain an important part of Creek culture today.

Ball play or Pokkecheta

Summary

Some time after 1,000 B.C. the Indians of the Chattahoochee River Valley developed a pattern of daily life that lasted, with little alteration, until European contact and the development of the deer hide trade in the 17th century, a period of about 2,500 years. It was a way of life that was rooted in and that grew out of the local environment, made possible by certain technological developments.

Among the latter was the development of pottery, which made possible the widespread exploitation of forest resources, particularly nuts and acorns, and enabled the people to prepare nourishing soups and stews much more easily; the discovery or perfection of the bow and arrow, which greatly increased the efficiency of hunters (and the deadliness of warfare); the acquisition and, probably, the codification, of a body of woodland knowledge, sometimes called primary forest efficiency by anthropologists, which we have touched upon in the chapters dealing with the "Wilderness School"; the development of village life, made possible, in large measure, by the foregoing; and a marked elaboration in social and spiritual life that manifested itself in artistic symbols and ritual paraphernalia. When domestic agriculture and corn culture were added to these elements during the first millennium A.D., the already existing way of life was further strengthened.

As related earlier, the trader James Adair said the Indians of the Southeast sometimes referred to this traditional way of life as "the old beloved path."

It is important to realize that the old beloved path was based upon a subsistence economy, not a surplus one. That is, the people took from nature only that which was necessary to survive. Waste was little tolerated, and a surplus of food meant only enough to last for a few weeks or, at most, through the winter months.   It was a way of life based upon respect for the environment, which supplied the necessities of life, and upon a belief system that emphasized harmony with nature.   Humankind lived in nature, not apart from or above it.   To do the latter was to commit the ultimate sin and to indulge a hubris certain to bring divine retribution.

By all accounts, the Indians of the Valley were a deeply spiritual people.   Yet, it would be too much to call this spirituality a religion in the formal sense.   To the early people of the Valley, religion was primarily a feeling, not a theology. Because they daily dwelt in nature and saw firsthand its mystery and power, Valley Indians thought of themselves as very small objects in an enormous and sometimes threatening universe. Consequently, they lived in awe of the world around them, fearful lest they offend the forces of nature and bring ruin upon themselves and their loved ones.

As we have seen, they were particularly sensitive to the possibility of offending the spirits of the animals upon whom they depended for meat and clothing.   To offset the hostility of the animal spirits, humankind needed a mediative medium.   That medium was plants or the vegetable kingdom.   Plant medicines not only helped cure diseases, most of which the people believed were caused by animals, but they also helped purify the body and mind so that an individual would be prepared to receive visions from the spiritual world.   These visions most often came in the form of dreams.

To the native people of the Valley, the difference between the waking and sleeping worlds was not so clear as we think it is today.   Dreams had enormous power over people's lives and were regarded as inherently revelatory.   Valley Indians were frequently guided in the conduct of their daily affairs by dreams, much as some people today are influenced by the position of certain stars.   They made war and arranged peace on the basis of dreams.   A warrior who had received a bad omen in a dream could abandon the warpath without disgrace. And there are tales, probably accurate, of Indians literally being frightened to death by their dreams. When they were going to sleep, Creek Indians did not say "Good night" they said, "I go to hunt a dream."

Yet for all their spirituality, the life of the average Indian of the Valley was hard and short and full of danger. It was a life lived largely out-of-doors, exposed to the heat of the sun and the raw elements of nature. No wonder the native people of the Valley venerated the sun and had such respect for the wind, thunder, and lightning. They made gods of natural forces because natural forces had such power over their lives.

The great river Chattahoochee, with its cooling, cleansing waters and its wild menagerie of fish, reptiles, amphibians, and shellfish, must have seemed like a god to the Indians. They spent much of their lives bathing in its limpid pools, fishing in its rocky runs, exploring its numerous tributaries, and hunting on the ridges and hills that guarded its flanks. For the native people of the Valley, the river was a primal force that both gave life and took it away. They knew its moods and seasons, felt the enormous power in its deep current, heard its roar, and experienced its anger when it was swollen by winter rains or when it jumped its banks in the spring runoff.

If you would know the early people of the Valley better, you must search for them in their river home. You will find them in the sun-dappled canebrakes on the river banks and in the shadowy, black-water swamps, thick with vines and roaring with the drone of mosquitoes. You will find them in the melancholy light of a winter afternoon on the river and in the earth-smell of a handful of clay. They are in the absurd squawk of the great blue heron and in the brilliant white slash of an egret probing in the bright green marsh grass. You will find them in the muscular suppleness of a water moccasin and in the pounding, contrapuntal rhythm of the nightheart, throbbing with the calls of frogs and toads and pierced from time to time with the unearthly cry of the bobcat and the shrieks of the dreaded owls.

They are with you when you swat at the droves of ever-present mosquitoes that swarm over the river in the hot months or when you marvel at the light caught in the branches of the sycamore trees on the river's banks. They are in the silvery leaves of the river birches whipped by the wind. They look upward with you at the silently circling black buzzards, now rising on the thermal winds, now spiraling steadily downward. They can be found in the deep, dusky green river on a hot summer day. The same water that laves you laved them. They are in the great thunderheads rolling in over the river and the sudden fury of the frontal storms, crackling with lightning and growling with thunder. Every time you hear the chilling rattle of the canebrake rattlesnake in the grass, they are with you. You will find them consorting with the catfish in the river's depths and with the alligators sunning themselves on the banks.

They can be found in the loud thwack of a beaver slapping its tail on the water, the rustling sound that comes from the cane stalks in the wind, the sibilant hissing of the rain on the river, the drumming noise the rain makes on the summer leaves. You will find them in the whistling hiss the alligator gar makes when it surfaces in the darkness and the metallic glint of a shad's body deep down in the water. Especially they are in the soughing of the wind through the pines, the beady eye and mighty wing-spread of the eagle, the tantalizing smell of wood smoke, the dry whistle of the deer in the deep woods, the singing of a hot fire on a winter's night, the sight of a long V of geese soaring overhead, the millions of stars in the night sky above the Chattahoochee. They said they would be in the stars. Look for them there.

BIBLIOGRAPHY

There are no texts that deal solely with daily life among the Indians of the Chattahoochee River Valley. Therefore what follows is a discussion of a variety of sources, ranging from archaeological surveys to anthropological studies and including personal narratives and my own field research among persons with an extensive knowledge of woodlore and with woodland skills relevant to the native American inhabitants of this area.

Although the text itself is divided into the Early Prehistoric Period, Middle Prehistoric, and Late Prehistoric Period, I have separated the bibliography according to sources on the prehistoric and historic Indians hoping this will simplify the process of locating a particular reference. I have tried not to list purely historical sources unless I found them to contain information relevant to the daily life of the Indians of the Valley. Many excellent bibliographies of historical sources are already available.

A complete bibliographical listing of all references used in compiling *The Old Beloved Path* follows the notes.

Notes on Prehistoric Sources

Although it is now dated, perhaps the best general introduction to North American archaeology remains the first volume of Gordon R. Willey's *An Introduction to American Archaeology* (1966). Jesse D. Jennings' *Prehistory of North America* (1980) is also useful. Brian M. Fagan's *The Great Journey: The Peopling of Ancient America* (1987) is a popular treatment of the earliest people in the Americas. There are many other general texts on the archaeology of the Americas, too many to list here, which a beginning student might wish to consult. Check with your local library.

There are no texts devoted specifically to the archaeology of

216

the prehistoric period in the Chattahoochee River Valley, John A. Walthall's *Prehistoric Indians of the Southeast: Archaeology of the Alabama and Middle South* (1980) is an excellent study that includes sections on the Chattahoochee River Valley. *Early Georgia* (1976), edited by Marilyn Pennington, it is entirely devoted to Georgia prehistory. It contains a number of valuable articles, listed separately in the bibliography that follows, and is highly recommended for an overview. Among these articles, Frank T. Schnell's "The Woodland Period South of the Fall Line" is particularly relevant.

Frank T. and Gail S. Schnell's and Vernon J. Knight, Jr.'s *Cemochechobee: Archaeology of a Mississippian Ceremonial Center on the Chattahoochee River* (1981) is site-specific, but contains a good deal of essential and authoritative information on the prehistory of the Valley. *Mississippian Settlement Patterns* (1978), edited by Bruce D. Smith, contains a wealth of information about that era in North American prehistory.

Beyond these books, the primary sources of information on the early people of the Chattahoochee River Valley are scholarly papers and impoundment surveys. Of particular interest is Joseph R. Caldwell's "Trend and Tradition in the Prehistory of the Eastern United States" (1958). Also helpful are Charles H. Fairbanks' "Creek and Pre-Creek" (1952); James B. Griffin's "Eastern North American Archaeology: A Summary" (1967); and Bruce D. Smith's "The Archaeology of the Southeastern United States: From Dalton to de Soto, 10,500-500 B.C." (1986). Overview in Time and Space" (1975). David W. Chase's "Background of the Archaeology of the Middle Chattahoochee Valley" (n.d.) and "The Averett Culture" (1959) also contain useful information.

More site-specific are the aforementioned *Cemochechobee* and Joseph R. Caldwell's "Investigations at Rood's Landing, Stewart County, Georgia" (1955); David L. DeJarnette's *Archaeological Salvage in the Walter F. George Basin of The Chattahoochee River in Alabama* (1975); David J. Hally's "Platform Mounds and the Nature of Mississippian Chiefdoms"

(1987); *Archaeological Investigations in the West Point Dam Area: A Preliminary Report* (1972) by Harold A. Huscher et al; "The Mandeville Site in Southwest Georgia" (1962) by James H. Kellar, A.R. Kelly, and Edward V. McMichael; A.R. Kelly's *A Preliminary Report on Archaeological Explorations At Macon, Georgia* (1938); *Walter F. George Lake: Archaeological Survey of the Fee Owned Lands Alabama and Georgia* (1984) by Vernon J. Knight Jr. and Tim S. Mistovich; Edward V. McMichael's and James H. Kellar's *Archaeological Salvage in the Oliver Basin* (1960); *Prehistory of the Middle Chattahoochee River Valley* (1989-90) by New South Associates in Stone Mountain; William H. Sears' *"Excavations At Kolomoki: Final Report"* (1956); and Gordon R. Willey's and William H. Sears' "The Kasita Site" (1952).

The most recent study of the Southeastern Ceremonial Complex is *The Southeastern Ceremonial Complex: Artifacts and Analysis* (1989), edited by Patricia Galloway. *Sun Circles and Human Hands: The Southeastern Indians Art and Industries* (1957) by Emma Fundaburke and Mary Douglas Foreman contains material relevant to the Southeastern Ceremonial Complex as well as numerous photographs and drawings of Southern Indians and their art work.

Two excellent juvenile booklets covering the prehistoric period in Georgia and Alabama are *Frontiers in the Soil: The Archaeology of Georgia* (1979) by Roy S. Dickens, Jr. and James L. McKinley, and Christine Adcock Wimberly's *Exploring Prehistoric Alabama Through Archaeology* (1980).

Historic Sources
As explained in the introduction, many historic sources were used in trying to understand daily life among the Indians of the Southeast and the Chattahoochee River Valley in late prehistoric times.   Among early Spanish sources consulted were "The Narrative of Alvar Nunuz Cabeza De Vaca," in *Spanish Explorers in the Southern United States* (1907), edited by F.W. Hodge and T.H. Lewis, reprinted in 1971; *Narratives of the*

Career of Hernando de Soto in the Conquest of Florida, as Told by a Knight of Elvas and in a Relation by Luys Hernandez de Biedma, Factor of the Expedition (1922), edited by Edward Gaylord Bourne, Buckingham Smith translation, reprinted 1973; and *The Florida of the Inca* (1951) by Garcilaso de la Vega, translated and edited by John Grier Varner and Jeannette Johnson Varner. Although the above texts were the most useful primary sources on the first contact between Indians of our area and Europeans, other useful sources were "The Expedition of Marcos Delgado from Apalache to the Upper Creek Country in 1686" (1937) by Mark F. Boyd; and *First Encounters: Spanish Explorations in the Caribbean and the United States, 1492-1570* (1989), edited by Jerald T. Milanich and Susan Milbrath.

The best general work on the Indians of the Southeast remains John R. Swanton's *The Indians of the Southeastern United States* (1946), reprinted numerous times, most recently in 1978. Swanton had an exhaustive list of sources from which to draw, including the early Spanish, French, and English explorers and soldiers, and I have used his work almost as if it were a primary source. For this reason, I have not broken out all the Spanish source material here. The reader may refer to Swanton in the bibliography for a full listing.

Swanton's work is particularly strong on the details of home manufacture, the uses of plants, hunting techniques, the preparation of game, and other aspects of daily life among the Creeks, Cherokee, Choctaw, Chickasaw, and many other Southern tribes.

Charles M. Hudson's *The Southeastern Indians* (1976) is an excellent and highly readable synthesis of the political, social, and religious life of the Indians of this region. It contains much information of value on the daily lives of native Americans of the Southeast, including the Creeks. Although authoritative and scholarly, it is a work of the heart as well as the mind and thus is especially valuable to anyone who wants to understand the Indians as people.

Some earlier general works on Southeastern Indians that are

of special interest include James Adair's *The History of the American Indians* (1775), which, despite its title, is exclusively about the Indians of the Southeastern United States and contains much information about their daily life. There are several more recent editions. It is well worth the effort to locate. So are the works of John and William Bartram. The latter's *Travels Through North and South Carolina, Georgia, East and West Florida* (1791) is available in a handsome re-issue by the Beehive Press (1973). See also John Bartram's *"Diary of a Journey Through the Carolinas, Georgia, and Florida from July 1, 1765, to April 10, 1766"* (1942).

The Creeks

Any serious study of the Creeks or Muskogulgi of this area must begin with the works of John R. Swanton, the late Smithsonian anthropologist. Among Swanton's works on the Creeks, all published by the U.S. Government Printing Office in Washington, D.C., are *Early History of the Creek Indians and Their Neighbors* (1922), which contains much of the information found in the massive *Forty-second Annual Report of the Bureau of American Ethnology (1924-25)*; and *Myths and Tales of the Southeastern Indians* (1929). All of these works are highly recommended. Swanton's "Tokulki of Tulsa" (1922, reissued 1974), an interpretation of the life of a young Alabama Creek, is still of interest.

Almost as valuable as Swanton's work is Albert S. Gatschet's *A Migration Legend of the Creek Indians with a Linguistic, Historic and Ethnographic Introduction* (1884, reprinted 1969). See also the same author's "Towns and Villages of the Creek Confederacy in the XVIII and XIX Centuries" (1901).

The best on-the-spot observations are those of Benjamin Hawkins, Superintendent of Indian Affairs in the South from 1796 to 1816. Hawkins knew the Creeks of the Valley better than any educated outsider of his time. His *Letters, Journals and Writings*, as edited in two volumes by C.L. Grant (1980), are essential primary sources. There have been numerous editions of Hawkins' description of the Creek towns and villages on the Chattahoochee and the Coosa and Tallapoosa rivers. The one I own is *The Creek Country* (1938). A more recent edition is *A Sketch of the Creek Country in the Years 1798 and 1799* (1971). See also Hawkins' biography by Merritt Bloodworth Pound, *Benjamin Hawkins, Indian Agent* (1951). The Georgia Historical Society in Savannah holds many priceless Hawkins papers and manuscripts.

Insight into the workings of the Indian mind can be found in Theron A. Nunez, Jr.'s "Creek Nativism and the Creek War of 1813-14" (1958). Nunez's article includes the complete recollections of George Stiggins, whose mother was a Natchez, and shows how deeply many Creeks opposed Benjamin Hawkins' attempts to "civilize" them. R. David Edmunds' *The Shawnee Prophet* (1985), goes into even more detail on the Indians' resistance to white men's ways. See also *The White Path* (1965) by W.E.S. Folsom-Dickerson.

Sacred Revolt (1991) by Joel W. Martin will deepen the reader's knowledge of Creek religion, mores and culture in almost every respect. It will also help explain why they no longer live in the Chattahoochee River Valley. Highly recommended. An invaluable recent addition to Creek studies is William C. Sturtevant's *A Creek Source Book* (1987), which contains numerous authoritative articles on Creek life which were used in the preparation of *The Old Beloved Path*. Of special worth are J.B. Hewitt's "Notes on the Creek Indians" (1987) and several articles by Frank G. Speck, including "The Creek Indians of Taskigi Town" (1987) and "Ceremonial Songs of the Creek and Yuchi Indians" (1987). Unfortunately, *A Creek Source Book* is quite an expensive volume. Donald E. Green's *The Creek People* (1973) is short but useful.

Several historical works contain valuable information on the Creeks and their social and political organization. Among these are *The Creek Frontier, 1540-1783* (1967) by David H. Corkran, and Angie Debo's *The Road to Disappearance* (1941, reissued

1967). Two works by Grant Foreman are essential to placing the Creeks in relation to other Indian people and to understanding some of the social forces that led to Removal. These are *The Five Civilized Tribes* (1934, reissued 1974), and *Indian Removal: The Emigration of the Five Civilized Tribes of Indians* (1932, reissued 1953 and 1976).

In addition to the Bartrams, already mentioned, a surprising number of Europeans and early Americans traveled through or rusticated in the Creek Nation before Removal. Unfortunately, most of them passed through the Chattahoochee River Valley long after the breakup of the old Indian way of life, and few tarried long enough to get to know the Indians well. Nevertheless there is some valuable observation on Indian manners in Louis LeClerc Milfort's *Memoirs; or, A Cursory Glance at My Different Travels and My Sojourn in the Creek Nation* (1802, new edition 1972). Milfort should be read with caution. Caleb Swan's "Position and State of Manners and Arts in the Creek, or Muscogee Nation in 1791" (1977) can be found in Schoolcraft. *Woodward's Reminiscences* (1859, reprinted 1929) by Thomas S. Woodward is an old Indian fighter's recollections.

For a more detailed bibliography on Creek sources, see the source list following or consult *The Creeks: A Critical Bibliography* (1979) by Michael D. Green.

Yuchi (and Others)

The best sources I have found on the Yuchi are Frank G. Speck's *Ethnology of the Yuchi Indians* (1909) and "The Yuchi: Children Of The Sun" (1959-60) by Carolyn Thomas Foreman. Swanton's works, particularly *The Indians of the Southeastern United States*, contains considerable information on the Yuchi and other Valley tribes, such as the Hitchiti and Apalachicola. Generally, the Hitchiti, a very important people in our region, are underrepresented in anthropological literature.

For an entirely different view of the Yuchi, see Joseph B. Mahan's *The Secret: America in World History before Columbus*.

Mythology

John R. Swanton's *Myths and Tales of the Southeastern Indians* (1929) is the basic text. It contains stories from the Creek, Yuchi, Alabama, Koasati, and Natchez people. Much of Swanton's material was based on stories collected by LaGrange lawyer W.O. Tuggle. For these and other interesting tales see *Shem, Ham & Japheth: The Papers of W.O. Tuggle* (1973), edited by Eugene Current-Garcia. George E. Lankford's *Native American Legends: Southeastern Legends* (1987) is an excellent study that contains an analysis of the material. *The Trickster: A Study in American Indian Mythology* (1956) by Paul Radin is an old classic that addresses the function of the trickster rabbit in Indian tales. It contains C.G. Jung's short essay on that subject. Frank G. Speck's "The Creek Indians of Taskigi Town" and J. B. Hewitt's "Notes on the Creek Indians," both of which can be found in *A Creek Source Book*, contain myths. I have also drawn upon a few tales collected by Albert S. Gatschet in "Some Mythic Stories of the Yuchi Indians" (1893).

An excellent book dealing with Southern Indian tales, including many from the native inhabitants of the Chattahoochee River Valley, is *Southern Indian Myths and Legends* (1985), edited by Virginia Pounds Brown and Laurella Owens. It will appeal to all ages.

Crafts, Games

There are disappointingly few works dealing with Southern Indian crafts and games. The best and most authoritative are the studies done by various Smithsonian anthropologists. John R. Swanton's *The Indians of the Southeastern United States* has already been mentioned. Stewart Culin's "Games of the North American Indians" (1907) in the *Twenty-Fourth Annual Report of the Bureau of American Ethnology* is a solid introduction to that subject. W. H. Holmes' "Aboriginal Pottery of the Eastern United States" (1903) in the *Twentieth Annual Report of the Bureau of American Ethnology*, is the standard reference. *Handbook of American Indians North of Mexico* (1912) by

Frederick Webb Hodge is still worth reading. It contains brief but authoritative discussions of such subjects as Indian games, crafts, mythology, and fire making. See also Lynn Barnes' "Creek Basketry" (1984).

Insight into the mythological or spiritual underpinnings of the ball play can be gleaned from a translation of Father Deutero Paiva's manuscript that appears in John Hann's *Apalachee: The Land Between The Rivers* (1988).

While arrows are relatively easy to manufacture from native materials such as river cane and dogwood, bows are another matter. They require patience and experience in working the wood, which was primarily black locust among the Indians of the Chattahoochee River Valley. D.C. Waldorf's *The Art of Making Primitive Bows and Arrows* (1985) is a detailed manual based on the use of Western woods. Its techniques, however, are applicable to woods available in our region.

Of numerous works on curing and tanning hides, see James Churchill's *The Complete Book of Tanning Skins and Furs* (1983), and the works of Albert B. Farnham, including *Home Manufacture Of Furs and Skins* and *Home Tanning And Leather Making Guide*. As is explained in the text, Southern Indians did not tan their hides as early whites did. The reader will have to work to extract data from these books that is relevant to the practices of Southeastern Indians.

Among juvenile books on Indian crafts, see W.E. McIntosh and Harvey Shell's *Indian Craft* (1987); *American Indian Habitats: How to Make Dwellings and Shelters with Natural Materials* (1975) by Nancy Simon and Evelyn Wolfson; and Allan A. MacFarlan's *A Book of American Indian Games* (1958). John L. Squires' and Robert E. McLean's *American Indian Dances* (1963) might be useful to high school teachers.

I benefitted greatly from conversations with contemporary masters of Indian crafts and wilderness skills. Chief among these has been Ben Kirkland of Albany, Georgia, who demonstrated fire-making, arrow-manufacture, and other aspects of native technologies. Preston Roberts of Hayes, North

Carolina, patiently demonstrated the Indian method of making buckskin, including fleshing of the hide, curing, and manufacture into clothing. Thomas White of Rydal, Georgia, showed me how to make projectile points and demonstrated his expertise with the blow gun. Driver Pheasant of Cherokee, North Carolina, demonstrated the blow gun and described how blow gun darts are made. Taema Tiger, a Yuchi Indian from Oklahoma, showed me a beautiful set of ball sticks which he made from hickory in the traditional way and explained their manufacture. His wife demonstrated tortoise shell leg rattles and explained how they were made. In a memorable evening on the Chattahoochee River, Gary White Deer, a Choctaw ceremonialist, explained to me the living tradition of the great plant medicines of the Indians of the Southeast. All of these people are living sources on the wilderness technologies, crafts, and spiritual life of the Indians of the Southeast, including those who used to make their homes in the Chattahoochee River Valley.

Plant Life, Wood Lore

Again, see Swanton, who devotes considerable space to both domestic and medicinal uses of plants by the Southeastern Indians and to Indian woodcraft generally.   As a general introduction to the subject, also see *American Indian Medicine* by Virgil J. Vogel (1970).

Despite its rather formidable title, Lewis H. Larson's *Aboriginal Subsistence Technology on the Southeastern Coastal Plain during the Late Prehistoric Period* (1980) is a very readable and quite excellent text.   It contains studies of the Indian methods of utilizing both fauna and flora. The section of Larson's work dealing with the Pine Barrens is a valuable commentary on the lower Chattahoochee River Valley, and his analysis of the principal Coastal Plains oaks and their acorns was very useful.

Although it deals with Midwestern flora, a helpful paper was Melvin Randolph Gilmore's "Uses of Plants by the Indians of the

Missouri River Region" (1919) in the *Twenty-Third Annual Report of the Bureau of American Ethnology.* This is one of the few works containing clear photographs of plants used by native Americans. Michael A. Weiner's *Earth Medicine-Earth Foods: Plant Remedies, Drugs, and Natural Foods of the North American Indians* (1972) was useful.

Of the numerous general works now available on edible wild plants, the most useful was Lee Allen Peterson's *A Field Guide to Edible Wild Plants: Eastern and Central North America* (1977) and Thomas S. Elias and Peter A. Dykeman's *Field Guide to North American Edible Wild Plants* (1982). In the Tom Brown series of wilderness books, see *Tom Brown's Guide To Wild Edible and Medicinal Plants* (1985). *Eat The Weeds* (1971) by Ben Charles Harris was also helpful.

The finest book on wood lore in the Southeast remains Horace Kephart's *Camping and Woodcraft* (1917, reissued 1971). Kephart is good on every aspect of living off the wilderness, but he is particularly thorough in his treatment of woods, plants and shelter.

I should also mention Bradford Angier's *Living Off The Wilderness* (1968), an excellent general text on wilderness survival that contains a particularly fine section on fire building.

Other works I benefitted from reading were Michael A. Godfrey's *A Sierra Club Naturalist's Guide to the Piedmont* (1980), and *Eastern Forests* (1985) by Ann and Myron Sutton. The best identification manual for trees found in the Valley is *The Audubon Society Field Guide to North American Trees: Eastern Region* (1980) by Elbert L. Little.

GENERAL BIBLIOGRAPHY
PREHISTORIC

Brannon, P. A. "Aboriginal Remains in the Middle Chattahoochee Valley of Alabama and Georgia." *American Anthropological* ll, no. 2 (1909). Reprint Lancaster, Pa.: New Era Publishing Co.

Caldwell, Joseph R. "Comment on the Papers." *Early Georgia* 3, no. 1 (1976):68-72.

_____. "Investigation at Rood's Landing, Stewart County, Georgia." *Early Georgia* 2, no. 1 (1955):22-47.

_____. "Trend and Tradition in the Prehistory of the Eastern United States." *American Anthropological Association Memoir 88*, 1958.

Chase, David W. "The Averett Culture." *Coweta Memorial Association Papers* 1. Columbus, Ga., 1959.

_____. "Background of the Archaeology of the Middle Chattahoochee Valley, 1955-63." Unpublished paper. Columbus, Ga.: Columbus Museum, n.d.

DeJarnette, David L. *Archaeological Salvage in the Walter F. George Basin of the Chattahoochee River in Alabama.* Historic Chattahoochee Commission. University, Al.: The University of Alabama Press, 1975.

DePratter, Chester B. "The Archaic in Georgia." *Early Georgia* 3, no. 1 (1976):1-16.

Dickens, Roy S., Jr., and James L. McKinley. *Frontiers in the Soil: The Archaeology of Georgia.* Chapel Hill, N.C.: Frontiers Publishing Co., 1979.

Fagan, Brian M. *The Great Journey: The Peopling of Ancient America.* London: Thames and Hudson, 1987.

Fairbanks, Charles H. "Creek and Pre-Creek." In *Archaeology of the Eastern United States*, ed. James B. Griffin, pp. 285-300. Chicago: University of Chicago Press, 1952.

Fundaburke, Emma Lila, and Mary D. Fundaburke Foreman, eds. *Sun Circles and Human Hands: The Southeastern Indians Art and Industries*. Luverne, Ala., 1957.

Galloway, Patricia, ed. *The Southeastern Ceremonial Complex: Artifacts and Analysis*. Lincoln and London: University of Nebraska Press, 1989.

Garrow, Patrick H. "The Woodland Period North of the Fall Line." *Early Georgia* 3, no. 1 (1976):17-26.

Griffin, James B. "Eastern North American Archaeology: A Summary." *Science* 15 (1967):175-91.

Hally, David J. "The Mississippi Period." *Early Georgia* 3, no. 1 (1976):37-52.

_____. "Platform Mounds and the Nature of Mississippian Chiefdoms." Paper presented at the Southeastern Archaeological Conference. Charleston, S.C., 1987.

Jennings, Jesse D. *Prehistory of North America*. New York: McGraw- Hill, 1968.

Kellar, James H., A. R. Kelly, and Edward V. McMichael. "The Mandeville Site in Southwest Georgia." *American Antiquity* 27 (1962):336-355.

Kelly, A. R. "A Preliminary Report on Archaeological Explorations at Macon, Georgia." *Bureau of American Ethnology* Bulletin 119 (1938):1-68.

Knight, Vernon J., Jr. "Mississippian Ritual." Ph.D. dissertation, University of Florida, 1981.

Knight, Vernon J., Jr., and Tim S. Mistovich. *Walter F. George*

Lake: Archaeological Survey of Fee Owned Lands Alabama and Georgia. Report of Investigations 42, University of Alabama, 1984.

Larson, Lewis H. *Aboriginal Subsistence Technology on the Southeastern Coastal Plain during the Late Prehistoric Period.* Gainesville: University Presses of Florida, 1980.

McMichael, Edward V., and James H. Kellar. *Archaeological Salvage in the Oliver Basin.* University of Georgia Laboratory of Archaeology Series, Report No. 2. Athens, Ga., 1960.

Neasins, Sarah W., ed. *Foraging, Collecting, and Harvesting: Archaic Period Subsistence and Settlement in the Eastern Woodlands.* Southern Illinois University at Carbondale Occasional Paper No. 6. Carbondale, 1986.

New South Associates. *Prehistory of the Middle Chattahoochee River Valley* Vol. 1 & 2. Stone Mountain, Ga., 1989-90.

Russell, Margaret Clayton. "Lamar and the Creeks: An Old Controversy Revisited." *Early Georgia* 3, no. 1 (1976): 53-67.

Schnell, Frank T. "The Woodland Period South of the Fall Line." *Early Georgia* 3, no. 1 (1976):27-36.

Schnell, Frank T., Vernon J. Knight, Jr., and Gail S. Schnell. *Cemochechobee: Archaeology of a Mississippian Ceremonial Center on the Chattahoochee River.* Gainesville: University Presses of Florida, 1981.

Sears, William H. "Excavations at Kolomoki: Final Report." *University of Georgia Series in Anthropology Report No. 5.* Athens: University of Georgia Press, 1956.

Smith, Bruce D. "The Archaeology of the Southeastern United States: From Dalton to deSoto, 10,500-500 B.P." *Advances in World Archaeology* 5 (1986).

_____, ed. *Mississippian Settlement Patterns.* New York: Academic Press, 1978.

Sowell, John D., and Udo Volker Nowack. *Projectile Points of the Tri-Rivers Basin.* Dothan, Al.: Generic Press, 1990.

Walthall, John A. *Prehistoric Indians of the Southeast: Archaeology of Alabama and the Middle South.* University, Al.: University of Alabama Press, 1980.

Willey, Gordon R. *An Introduction to American Archaeology, Vol. One: North and Middle America.* Englewood Cliffs, N.J.: Prentice-Hall, 1966.

Willey, Gordon R., and William H. Sears. "The Kasita Site." *Southen Indian Studies* 4 (1952):3-18.

Wimberly, Christine Adcock. *Exploring Prehistoric Alabama Through Archaeology.* Birmingham, Al.: Explorer Books, 1980.

Yarbrough, Susan L. "A Brief Analysis of the Unionid (Mollusca- bivalvia) Remains from the Cannon Site, Crisp County, Ga." Unpublished paper. Columbus, Ga.: Columbus Museum, 1976.

HISTORIC

Adair, James. *The History of the American Indians.* 1775. New York: Johnson Reprint Corp., 1968.

Angier, Bradford. *Living Off the Country.* Harrisburg, Pa.: Stackpole Books, 1968.

Barnes, Lynn. "Creek Basketry." In *Basketry of Southeastern Indians*, Marshall Gettys, ed. Idabel, Ok.: Museum of the Red River, 1984.

Bartram, John. "Diary of a Journey through the Carolinas, Georgia, and Florida from July 1, 1765, to April 10, 1766." Francis Harper, ed. *Transactions of the American Philosophical Society*, n.s., 33, part 1 (1942):1-120.

Bartram, William. "Observations on the Creek and Cherokee Indians, 1789." *Transactions of the American Ethnological Society* 3, part 1 (1853):1-81.

_____. "Travels in Georgia and Florida, 1773-74: A Report to Doctor John Fothergill." *Transactions of the American Philosophical Society*, n.s., 33, part 2 (1943):121-242.

_____. *Travels Through North and South Carolina, Georgia, East and West Florida*. 1791. Savannah, Ga.: Beehive Press, 1973.

Beloin, Gerard. *The Firewood Efficiency Manual*. Colebrook, N.H.: Information, Inc., 1980.

Berry, James Berthold. *Southern Woodland Trees*. Chicago: World Book Co., 1924.

Bolton, Herbert E. "Spanish Resistance to the Carolina Traders in Western Georgia (1680-1704)." *Georgia Historical Quarterly* 9 (1925):115-30.

Bourne, Edward Gaylord, ed. *Narratives of the Career of Hernando de Soto in the Conquest of Florida, as Told by a Knight of Elvas and in a Relation by Luys Hernandez de Biedma, Factor of the Expedition*. Translated by Buckingham Smith. New York: Allentorn Book Co., 1922.

Boyd, Mark F. "The Expedition of Marcos Delgado from Apalache to the Upper Creek Country in 1686." *Florida Historical Quarterly* 16 and 17, no. 1 (1937):3-32.

Boyd, Mark F., Hale G. Smith, and John W. Griffin. *Here They Once Stood: The Tragic End of the Apalachee Missions.* Gainesville: University of Florida Press, 1951.

Brannon, Peter A. "Aboriginal Towns in Alabama." In *Handbook of the Alabama Antropological Society.*pp. 42-58. Montgomery, Al.: Brown Printing Co., 1920.

_____. *The Southern Indian Trade: Being Particularly a Study of Material from the Tallapoosa River Valley of Alabama.* Montgomery, Al.: Paragon Press, 1935.

Brockman, C. Frank. *Trees of North America.* New York: Golden Press, 1968.

Brown, Tom, Jr. *Tom Brown's Guide to Wild Edible and Medicinal Plants.* New York: Berkley Books, 1985.

Brown, Tom, Jr., with Judy Brown. *Tom Brown's Field Guide to Nature and Survival for Children.* New York: Berkley Books, 1985.

Brown, Virginia Pounds, and Laurella Owens, eds. *Southern Indian Myths and Legends.* Birmingham, Al.: Beechwood Books, 1985.

_____. *The World of Southern Indians.* Birmingham, Al.: Beechwood Books, 1983.

Broyles, Bettye J., ed. *Proceedings of the Twenty-Second Southeastern Archaeological Conference.* Southeastern Archaeological Conference, Bulletin 5, 1967.

Buckner, Henry Frieland. *A Grammar of the Maskwke or Creek Language*. G. Herrod, interp. Marion, Al.: Domestic and Indian Mission Board of the Southern Baptist Convention, 1860.

Churchill, James. *The Complete Book of Tanning Skins and Furs*. Harrisburg, Pa.: Stackpole Books, 1983.

Columbus, Georgia Department of Community Development Planning Division. *Natural Systems of Columbus, Georgia*. Columbus, Ga., 1978.

Corkran, David H. *The Creek Frontier 1540-1783*. Norman: University of Oklahoma Press, 1967.

Cotterill, Robert Spencer. *The Southern Indians: The Story of the Civilized Tribes Before Removal*. Norman: University of Oklahoma Press, 1954.

Crane, Verner Winslow. *The Southern Frontier, 1670-1732*. Durham, N.C.: Duke University Press, 1928. Ann Arbor: University of Michigan Press, 1929.

Crawford, Barrie F. *For the Love of Wildflowers*. Hamilton, Ga.: Buckeye Press, 1985.

Culin, Stewart. "Games of the North American Indians." *Twenty-fourth Annual Report of the Bureau of American Ethnology*. Washington, D.C.: Government Printing Office, 1907.

Cumming, William P. *The Southeast in Early Maps*. Princeton, N.J.: Princeton University Press, 1958.

Current-Garcia, Eugene, ed., with Dorohty B. Hatfield. *Shem, Ham & Japheth: The Papers of W. O. Tuggle*. Athens:

University of Georgia Press, 1973.

Debo, Angie. *The Road to Disappearance*. Norman: University of Oklahoma Press, 1941. New ed. 1967.

Dormon, Caroline. *Flowers Native to the Deep South*. Harrisburg, Pa.: Mount Pleasant Press, 1959.

Duncan, Wilbur H. *Guide to Georgia Trees*. Athens: University of Georgia Press, 1941.

Duncan, Wilbur H., and Leonard E. Foote. *Wildflowers of the Southeastern United States*. Athens: University of Georgia Press, 1975.

Edmunds, R. David. *The Shawnee Prophet*. Lincoln and London: University of Nebraska, 1985.

Elias, Thomas S., and Peter A. Dykeman. *Field Guide to North American Edible Wild Plants*. New York: Outdoor Life Books, 1982.

Farnham, Albert B. *Home Manufacture of Furs and Skins*. Columbus, Oh.: A. R. Harding, n.d.

_____. *Home Tanning and Leather Making Guide*. Columbus, Oh.: A. R. Harding, n.d.

Folsom-Dickerson, W. E. S. *The White Path*. San Antonio: The Naylor Co., 1965.

Foreman, Carolyn Thomas. "The Yuchi: Children of the Sun." *The Chronicles of Oklahoma*. (1959-60):480-501.

Foreman, Grant. *Indian Removal: The Emigration of the Five Civilized Tribes of Indians*. Norman: University of Oklahoma

Press, 1932. New ed., 1953. Reprinted, 1976.

_____. *The Five Civilized Tribes: Cherokee, Chickasaw, Choctaw, Creek, Seminole.* Intro. by John R. Swanton. Norman: University of Oklahoma Press, 1934. Reprinted, 1974.

Fretwell, Mark E. *Benjamin Hawkins in the Chattahoochee Valley: 1798.* West Point, Ga.: Valley Historical Association, 1954.

_____. *This So Remote Frontier: The Chattahoochee Country of Alabama and Georgia.* Tallahassee, Fla.: Historic Chattahoochee Commission, 1980.

Fundaburke, Emma Lila *Southeastern Indians: Life Portraits. A Catalogue of Pictures 1564-1860.* Luverne, Ala., 1958.

Gannon, Michael V. *The Cross in the Sand: The Early Catholic Church in Florida 1513-1870.* Gainesville: University of Florida Press, 1967.

Gatschet, Albert S. *A Migration Legend of the Creek Indians with a Linguistic, Historic, and Ethnographic Introduction.* 1884-88. New York: AMS Press, 1969.

_____. "Some Mythic Stories of the Yuchi Indians." *The American Anthropologist* 6 (1893):279-282.

_____. "Towns and Villages of the Creek Confederacy in the XVIII and XIX Centuries." *Report of the Alabama History Commission* 1 (1901):386-415.

Gilmore, Melvin Randolph. "Uses of Plants by the Indians of the Missouri River Region." *Twenty-third Annual Report of the Bureau of American Ethnology.* Washington, D.C.:

Government Printing Office, 1919.

Godfrey, Michael A. *A Sierra Club Naturalist's Guide to the Piedmont*. San Francisco: Sierra Club Books, 1980.

Grant, C. L., ed. *Letters, Journals, and Writings of Benjamin Hawkins, Vols. I & II*. Savannah, Ga.: Beehive Press, 1980.

Green, Donald E. *The Creek People*. Phoenix: Indian Tribal Series, 1973.

Green, Michael D. *The Creeks: A Critical Bibliography*. Bloomington and London: Indiana University Press, 1979.

Hall, Captain Basil. *Travels in North America in the Years 1827-1828*. 3 Vols. Edinburgh: Cadell, 1829.

Hall, Margaret Hunter (Mrs. Basil). *The Aristocratic Journey: Being the Outspoken Letter of Mrs. Basil Hall, Written during a Fourteen Months' Sojourn in America, 1827-1828*. Edited by Una Pope Hennessy. G.P. Putnam & Sons, 1831.

Hann, John H. *Apalachee: The Land Between the Rivers*. Gainesville: University of Florida Press, 1988.

Harris, Ben Charles. *Eat the Weeds*. Barre, Mass.: Barre Publishers, 1971.

Hawkins, Benjamin. *A Sketch of the Creek Country in the Years 1798 and 1799. Collections of the Georgia Historical Society* 3, part 1 (1848). Reprinted, New York: Kraus, 1971.

Hawkins, Col. Benjamin. *The Creek Country*. Americus, Ga.: Americus Book Co., 1938.

Hewitt, J. N. B. "Notes on the Creek Indians." *A Creek Source*

Book. New York and London: Garland Publishing, 1987.

Hodge, Frederick Webb, ed. *Handbook of American Indians North of Mexico.* Vols 1 and 2. Washington, D.C.: Government Printing Office, 1912.

Hodge, F. W. and T. H. Lewis, eds. "The Narritive of Alvar Nunez Cabeca de Vaca." *Spanish Explorers in the Southern United States, 1528-1543.* New York: Barnes & Noble, 1907. Reprinted 1971.

Holmes, W. H. "Aboriginal Pottery of the Eastern United States." *Twentieth Annual Report of the Bureau of American Ethnology.* Washington, D.C.: Government Printing Office, 1903.

Hudson, Charles M., ed. *Black Drink: A Native American Tea.* Athens: University of Georgia Press, 1979.

_____, ed. *Four Centuries of Southern Indians.* Athens: University of Georgia Press, 1975.

_____. "The Genesis of Georgia's Indians." *The Journal of Southwest Georgia History* 3, Fall, 1985.

_____, ed. *Red, White, and Black: Symposium on Indians in the Old South.* Southern Anthropological Society Proceedings, no. 5. Athens: University of Georgia Press, 1971.

_____. *The Southeastern Indians.* Knoxville: University of Tennessee Press, 1976.

Hudson, Charles M., Marvin T. Smith, and Chester B. DePratter. "The Hernando De Soto Expedition: From Apalachee to Chiaha." *Southeastern Archaeology* 3 (l),

Summer, 1984.

Huscher, Harold A. *Southern Indian Studies, Vol. XVI.* Chapel Hill: The Archaeological Society of North Carolina, 1964.

Huscher, Harold A. et al. *Archaeological Investigations in the West Point Dam Area: A Preliminary Report* Vols. I & II. Athens, Ga.: Laboratory of Archaeology, Department of Sociology and Anthropology, University of Georgia, 1972.

Jones, Samuel B., Jr. "The Flora and Phytogeography of the Pine Mountain Region of Georgia." *Castanea* 39 (1974):113-149.

Jones, Samuel B., Jr. and Nancy Craft Coile. *The Distribution of the Vascular Flora of Georgia.* Athens, Ga.: Department of Botany, University of Georgia, 1988.

Kephart, Horace. *Camping and Woodcraft: A Handbook for Vacation Campers and for Travelers in the Wilderness.* Vols. 1 & 2. New York: Macmillan Co., 1917.

Lankford, George E., ed. *Native American Legends: Southeastern Legends.* Little Rock, Ark.: August House, 1987.

Lewis, Thomas M. N., and Madeline Kneberg. *Tribes That Slumber: Indians of the Tennessee Region.* Knoxville: University of Tennessee Press, 1958.

Little, Elbert L. *The Audubon Society Field Guide to North American Trees: Eastern Region.* New York: Alfred A. Knopf, 1980.

Loughridge, Robert M., and David M. Hodge. *English and Muskogee Dictionary.* St. Louis: J. T. Smith, 1890.

Lower Chattahoochee Area Planning and Development Commission. *Economic Base Analysis of the Lower Chattahoochee Area*. Columbus, Ga., 1973.

_____. *Lower Chattahoochee Area Exisiting Land Use: Survey and Analysis, 1972*. Columbus, Ga., 1972.

_____. *Lower Chattahoochee Area Future Land Use: Survey and Analysis, 1972*. Columbus, Ga., 1972.

McIntosh, Chief W. E. "Dode," and Harvey Shell. *Indian Craft*. Happy Camp, Ca.: Naturegraph Publishers, 1987.

McKenney, Thomas L., and James T. Hall. *History of the Indian Tribes of North America, with Biographical Sketches and Anecdotes of the Principal Chiefs, Embellished with One Hundred and Twenty Portraits from the Indian Gallery in the Department of War, at Washington*. 3 vols. Philadelphia: Frederick W. Greenough, 1838-44. New ed., ed. Frederick W. Hodge, Edinburgh: J. Grant, 1933-34.

MacFarlan, Allan A. *Book of American Indian Games*. New York: Association Press, 1958.

Mahan, Joseph B. *The Secret: America in World History before Columbus*. Columbus, Ga.: Joseph B. Mahan, 1983.

Martin, Joel W. *Sacred Revolt: The Muskogee's Struggle for a New World*. Boston: Beacon Press, 1991.

Martin, John H. *Columbus, Georgia: From its Selection as a "Trading Town" in 1827 to its Partial Destruction by Wilson's Raid in 1865*. Columbus, Ga.: Thomas Gilbert, 1874. Reprint Easley, S.C.: Georgia Geneological Reprints, 1972.

Mason, Carol I. "Eighteenth Century Culture Change among the Lower Creeks." *Florida Anthropologist* 16 (1963):65-80.

Milanich, Jerald T. and Susan Milbrath, eds. *First Encounters: Spanish Explorations in the Caribbean and the United States, 1492-1570.* Gainesville: University of Florida Press, 1989.

Milfort, Louis LeClerc. *Memoirs: or, A Cursory Glance at My Different Travels and My Sojourn in the Creek Nation,* ed. John Francis McDermott, trans. Geraldine de Courcy. Originally published in French, 1802. Chicago: R. R. Donnelley, 1956. New ed., trans. and ed. Ben C. McCary, Savannah, Ga.: Beehive Press, 1972.

Mooney, James. *Myths of the Cherokee and Sacred Formulas of the Cherokees.* Nashville, Tenn.: Charles and Randy Elder, 1982.

Morgan, Robert T. *The Cantey Plantation and Fort Mitchell, Alabama.* Archaeological Monograph 7. Auburn, Ala.: Auburn University, 1983.

Nunez, Theron A., Jr. "Creek Nativism and the Creek War of 1813- 1814." *Ethnohistory* 5 (1958):1-47, 131-75, 292-301.

Opler, Morris E. "The Creek 'Town' and the Problem of Creek Indian Political Reorganization." In *Human Problems in Technological Change,* ed., Edward H. Spicer, pp. 165-80. New York: Russell Sage Foundation, 1952.

Owen, Marie Bankhead. "Indians in Alabama." *Alabama Historical Quarterly* 12 (1950):5-91.

Owen, Thomas M. "Alabama Indian Chiefs." *Alabama Historical Quarterly* 13 (1951):5-91.

_____. "Indian Tribes and Towns in Alabama." *Alabama Historical Quarterly* 12 (1950):118-241.

Pennignton, Edgar Legare, ed. "Some Ancient Georgia Indian Lore." *Georgia Historical Quarterly* 15 (1931):192-98.

Peterson, Lee Allen. *A Field Guide to Edible Wild Plants: Eastern and Central North America.* Boston: Houghton Mifflin Co., 1977.

Pound, Merritt Bloodworth. "Benjamin Hawkins, Indian Agent." *Georgia Historial Quarterly* 13 (1929):392-409.

_____. *Benjamin Hawkins, Indian Agent.* Athens: University of Georgia Press, 1951.

Radin, Paul. *The Trickster: A Study in American Indian Mythology.* with commentaries by Karl Kereny and C. G. Jung. New York: Philosophical Library, 1956.

Read, William A. *Indian Place Names in Alabama.* University, Ala.: University of Alabama Press, 1984.

_____. "Indian Stream Names in Georgia." *International Journal of American Linguistics* 15 (1949):128-132.

_____. "Indian Stream Names in Georgia II." *International Journal of American Linguistics* 16 (1950):203-207.

Simon, Nancy, and Evelyn Wolfson. *American Indian Habitats: How to Make Dwellings and Shelters with Natural Materials.* New York: David McKay Co., 1975.

Smith, Marvin T. *Archaeology of Aboriginal Culture Change in the Interior Southeast: Depopulation During The Early Historic Period.* Gainesville: University of Florida Press,

1987.

Speck, Frank G. "Ceremonial Songs of the Creek and Yuchi Indians." *A Creek Source Book.* New York and London: Garland Publishing, 1987.

_____. "The Creek Indians of Taskigi Town." *A Creek Source Book.* New York and London: Garland Publishing, 1987.

_____. *Ethnology of the Yuchi Indians.* Philadelphia: Anthropological Publication of the University Museum, University of Pennsylvania, 1909.

Squires, John L., and Robert E. McLean. *American Indian Dances.* New York: Ronald Press Co., 1963.

Sturtevant, William C., ed. *A Creek Source Book.* New York and London: Garland Publishing, 1987.

Sutton, Ann, and Myron Sutton. *Eastern Forests.* The Audubon Society Nature Guides. New York: Alfred A. Knopf, 1985.

Swan, Caleb. "Position and State of Manners and Arts in the Creek, or Muscogee Nation in 1791." In *Historical and Statistical Information Respecting the History, Condition and Prospects of the Indian Tribes of the United States,* Henry Rowe Schoolcraft 5 (1851-57):251-83.

Swanton, John R. *Early History of the Creek Indians and Their Neighbors.* Washington, D. C.: Government Printing Office, 1922.

_____. *Final Report of the United States de Soto Expedition Commission.* Washington, D. C.: Government Printing Office, 1939.

_____. *Forty-second Annual Report of the Bureau of American Ethnology to the Secretary of the Smithsonian Institution, 1924-1925.* Washington, D. C.: Government Printing Office, 1928.

_____. *The Indians of the Southeastern United States.* Washington, D. C.: Government Printing Office, 1946. Reprint 1978.

_____. *Myths and Tales of the Southeastern Indians.* Washington, D. C.: Government Printing Office, 1929.

_____. "Tokulki of Tulsa." In *American Indian Life*, ed. Elsie Clews Parsons, pp. 127-45. New York: B. W. Huebsch, 1922. Reprint Lincoln: University of Nebraska Press, 1974.

Taylor, Kathryn S., and Stephen F. Hamblin. *Handbook of Wild Flower Cultivation.* New York: MacMillan Co., 1963.

Telfair, Nancy. *A History of Columbus, Georgia: 1828-1928.* Columbus, Ga.: Historical Publishing, 1929.

Thomas, David Hurst, ed. *Columbian Consequences: Archaeological and Historical Perspectives on the Spanish Borderland East.* Vol. 2. Washington and London: Smithsonian Institute Press, 1990.

Twiggs, Gen. John. "The Creek Troubles of 1793." *Georgia Historical Quarterly* 11 (1927):274-280.

Utley, Francis Lee, and Marion R. Hemperley. *Placenames of Georgia: Essays of John H. Goff.* Athens: University of Georigia Press, 1975.

Varner, John Grier, and Jeannette Johnson Varner, eds. *The Florida of the Inca.* Austin: University of Texas Press, 1951.

Vogel, Virgil J. *American Indian Medicine.* Norman: University of Oklahoma Press, 1970.

Walden, Howard T. *Native Inheritance: The Story of Corn in America.* New York and London: Harper & Row, 1966.

Waldorf, D. C. *The Art of Making Primitive Bows and Arrows.* Branson, Mo.: Mound Builder Books, 1985.

Walker, Anne Kendrick. *Russell County in Retrospect: An Epic of the Far Southeast.* Richmond, Va.: Dietz Press, 1950.

Weatherford, Jack. *Indian Givers: How the Indians of the Americas Transformed the World.* New York: Crown Publishers, 1988.

Weiner, Michael A. *Earth Medicine-Earth Foods: Plant Remedies, Drugs, and Natural Foods of the North American Indians.* New York: Collier Books, 1972.

Williams, Walker L., ed. *Southeastern Indians Since the Removal Era.* Athens: University of Georgia Press, 1979.

Winn, Bill. "Creek Indians of the Chattahoochee Valley." A series of 21 articles from *The Columbus Ledger-Enquirer,* May 14, 1989-October 1, 1989, with two columns from June 12 & 26, 1988. Columbus, Ga.

_____. *The First Georgians: A Series of Ten Articles written for and published by The Atlanta Journal.* Columbus, Ga.: Columbus Junior Woman's Club, 1968.

Woodward, Thomas S. *Woodward's Reminiscences of the Creek, or Muscogee Indians, Contained in Letters to Friends in Georgia and Alabama.* Montgomery, Al.: Barrett and Wimblish, 1859. New ed. Tuscaloosa, Al.: Alabama Book

Store, 1929.

Worsley, Etta Blanchard. *Columbus on the Chattahoochee.* Columbus, Ga.: Columbus Office Supply, 1951.

Wright, J. Leitch, Jr. *Creeks & Seminoles: The Destruction and Regeneration of the Muscogulge People.* Lincoln and London: University of Nebraska Press, 1986.

Young, Mary E. *Redskins, Ruffleshirts, and Rednecks: Indian Allotments in Alabama and Mississippi, 1830-1860.* Norman: University of Oklahoma Press, 1961.

An excellent new introduction to the land of the Creeks is Robbie Ethridge's *Creek Country: The Creek Indians and Their World* (2003). It contains a wealth of interesting information. H. Thomas Foster II's *Archaeology of the Lower Muskogee Creek Indians, 1715-1836* (2007) is well worth reading for those interested in acquiring a more detailed understanding of the archaeology of the principal historic native occupants of the Lower Chattahoochee River Valley. It contains a very good section on botanical remains by Mary Theresa Bonhage-Freund and Lisa O'Steen. Kathryn E. Holland Braund's much admired *Deerskins & Duffels: Creek Indian Trade with Anglo-America, 1685-1815* (1993) is an essential and well-written text on an important facet of Creek life.

INDEX

A-cee, Black drink (*Ilex vomitoria*), 124, 130, 147, 153-157, 210; associated with *Yahola,* 167; great medicine, 180; in *Poskeeta,* 209; *illus.,* 184

A-cee yahola, black drink singer, i.e., Osceola, 156, 196

Abercrombie mound, 102

Abihka, 125, 143

Abortifacient, 185

Abortions, 192

Acheena. See cedar

Acorn, *lokcha:* 30; bread and oil, 64; in fall, 20, 81; importance of pottery, 28; important oak species, 19; leaching, 17, 28; meal, 21; at Rood's, 105

Adair, James, 212

Adena culture, 37, 44

Adornos, 105, 111, 118

Adultery, 197

Adults, 110, 111, 194

Adzes, 21

Agriculture: beans, 92, 105; beginnings in Woodland, 37, 43, 63-64, 70; bottomlands, 19; communal fields, 93, 198; corn culture in Mississippian period, 91-94; early cultigens, 63-64; edible wild plants, 16-17, 50-66, garden patches, 93, 95; of Middle American origin, 37; Mississipian sites, 91; seeds and the beginning of, 63-64; squash, 63, 64, 92; subsistence, 47; vegetables, 47-52, 110. *See* corn, plants, sunflowers

Alabama, 31, 32

Alabama Indians, 128, 141

Alabama Piedmont, 6

Alabama River, 32

Alabama shad (*A. alabamae*), 68

Alder, 73

Alektchulgi, Creek physicians, 171, 172, 187. *See* disease and cure

Alligator, *halpata,* (*Alligator mississippiensis*), 68-69, 168

Alligator clan, 140, 141

Altar, 113, 115

Altithermal interval, 14

Amaranths (*Amaranthus spp.*), 51, 63, 64

American beech (*Fagus grandifolia*), 18, 30, 49; nuts, 64, 72

American holly, *essee-faskee* (*Ilex opaca*), 73

American lotus (*Nelumbo lutea*), 52, 62

American shad (*Alosa*